Dumb . . .

Did you hear about the dumb father who got up and struck a match to see if he had blown out the candle?

Dumber . . .

Jasper and Newton were walking through the outskirts of town when they spotted a human head lying in the road. Jasper picked the head up and held it high in the air to see it better.

"Golly!" he cried, "it looks like J.D. Bibb!"

"Naw!" said his buddy. "Ole J.D. was a much shorter guy!"

Dumbest . . .

The Grahams were riding on a scenic tour train for the first time. They brought bananas for lunch. Just as the husband bit into his banana, the train entered a tunnel. "Did you take a bite of your banana?" he asked his wife.

"No."

"Well, don't!" exclaimed Graham. "I did, and I went blind!"

LARRY WILDE

The Dumb, Dumber, Dumbest Joke Book

PINNACLE BOOKS

KENSINGTON PUBLISHING CORP.

To Hershel Peak
The smartest guy I know

Stupid is as stupid does.
      —FORREST GUMP

Contents

Introduction

This book is strictly about dimwits, dweezils and dumbbells. In other words, each and every one of us.

The ranks of the mentally challenged are not limited to those with single-digit IQs or serious education deficiencies. We've all said and done spectacularly stupid things—even (or perhaps most especially) college professors, politicians, doctors, scientists, business executives and sports figures.

Brash sportscaster Howard Cosell once suggested that most baseball players were "afflicted with tobacco-chewing mind." This from a man whose own mental faculties sometimes, critics claimed, weren't worth a bucket of spit.

Sports figures are notorious for making monumental verbal errors.

Casey Stengel, feisty manager of the Yankees and Mets, had a witless way with words:

"Good pitching always stops good hitting and vice versa."

But perhaps the all-time baseball brain surgeon was Yogi Berra. In presenting an award to Joe DiMaggio, he said, "Joe, I want to thank you for teaching me that the only way to do something correctly, is to do it right."

Other not-so-famous sports "lingoists" have made

some moronic mental pop-ups. This was heard on radio station KGO, San Francisco:

"Here's a bulletin just in. It's now official! Juan Pizzaro has just pissed a no-hit, no-run ball game."

And hockey fans get their share of yuks:
Did you hear about the Maple Leafs hockey player who went fishing?
He caught fifty pounds of ice.
And his wife drowned trying to cook it.

Of course, sports doesn't have a monopoly on dimwits, dweezils and dumbbells. Not when politics enters the picture:

Consider this current political hatpin making the rounds:
Why does Dolly Parton resent Newt Gingrich and Robert Dole?
Because they are the two biggest boobs in the country.

Dweezildom knows no professional boundries. Dumbbells are not limited by geography, age, looks, race, creed or sex. Dimwittedness is an equal opportunity affliction. Everybody is stupid, only about different things.
In Manhattan, lovers of moronic mirth say,
Irving is so stupid he has to dip his finger in a glass to see if he has a soft drink!

When he got out of kindergarten he was so excited he could hardly shave.

His elevator doesn't go to the top floor.

The light's on, but nobody's home.

In California's Silicon Valley one often hears references to the mega-muddlehead traits of computer nerds:
They don't make a chip small enough for his data bank.

He's got more gray matter in his whole head than most of us have in a pinky finger.

He has a forty-inch waist and an IQ to match!

He's a few french fries short of a Happy Meal.

Wander throughout the great state of Texas and you'll hear folks saying,
If brains were leather, Billy Bob couldn't saddle a flea.

He's a couple a pork chops shy of a barbecue.

Even if he had all his shit together, he still couldn't fertilize scrub.

And the Midwest has its share of ding-a-lings. Dimwits who inspire comments such as these:
Hank ain't the sharpest tool in the shed.

He hasn't enough sense to steer a horse around a merry-go-round.

He's got a kink in his hose.

His pizza hasn't been delivered.

And the Southeast makes a contribution:

Dick doesn't have both oars in the water.

His boat isn't tied securely to the pier.

If it was raining soup, he'd be out there with a knife and fork.

A while back Dumb Blonde Jokes were sweeping the country, mostly gags about women. Over the years there have been legions of jokes poking fun at females who were less than M.I.T. graduates—everyone from women drivers to farmers' daughters to mothers-in-law.

This time the jokes are on men. To repeat: dumbbellism is sexless. But if you must be politically correct, be my guest and switch the joke. You'll soon discover the knife cuts both ways. To paraphrase Casey Stengel, women can be just as stupid as men and vice versa.

Fortunately, there is one good thing about stupidity. You can be fairly sure that it is genuine.

LARRY WILDE
Carmel, California

Macho Muttonheads

"Say, your house is burning."
"That's okay. I got enough lumber in the attic to build a new one."

———

During a recent stock market dip an Indianapolis broker lost everything.

"I have no money to pay you, Mr. Kogen," he said to the plumber who had just presented a large bill. "In lieu of payment, will you take a Rembrandt?"

"If it has four good tires," said the plumber, "you got a deal!"

McAfee and Bracket were driving home after a big party.

"Hey," said McAfee, "be sure to watch out for that bridge that's coming down the road toward us."

"What are you telling me to 'watch out' for?" asked Brackett. "You're the one who's driving!"

———

Young Bradley arrived at his date's house wearing a shirt that had water dripping from it.

"What're you doin'?" asked his girlfriend. "How come your shirt is soakin' wet?"

"Well," said Bradley, "it said on the label: WASH AND WEAR."

———

Drakich and Cannell were havin' a beer at the famous Wyoming Nugget Bar & Grill.

"What'd you do today?" asked Drakich.

"I was laying linoleum," answered Cannell.

Drakich grinned. "She got a friend?"

Calvin went to Pearson's Pet Shop to complain that his canary wouldn't sing.

"File the beak just a little," said the owner, "and the bird will sing. But—if you file it too much, the canary will die."

Two weeks later Pearson ran into Calvin on the street and asked about his canary.

"He died," said Calvin.

"But I told you not to file the beak too much."

"I didn't," explained Calvin, "but by the time I got him out of the vise, he was already dead."

———

Guidry called in Plotke, the painter, for an estimate to paint his house.

"How much you gonna charge me?" asked Guidry.

"Twenty dollars an hour," replied Plotke.

"Good Lord!" exclaimed the home owner. "I wouldn't pay Michelangelo that price!"

"I tell you one thing, mister," said the painter. "If that guy you mentioned is doin' the job for less, he ain't no member of our union!"

Loomis: Does your dog have a license?
Fenton: Hell, no! I do all the drivin'.

—————

Delmer: How'd you like the play last night over at the
    high school?
Farley: I only seed the first act, but not the second.
Delmer: Why didn't you stay?
Farley: I couldn't wait that long. It said on the program,
    'Two Years Later.'

—————

Young Willis had several dates with Erlene but was
unable to make out. He asked his buddy Alvah what to
do.

"Jes' drive her out in the country," advised Alvah,
"and tell her to put out or get out."

So Willis got Erlene into his pickup truck, found a
secluded spot ten miles out of town and parked.

"Okay," said the boy, "now get out or I'll put you
out!"

—————

Did you hear about the dumb father who got up and
struck a match to see if he had blown out the candle?

Edney and Cole, two Ohio Edison electrical repairmen, were working on a blown house circuit.

"Hey, Cole!" said Edney. "See those two wires?"

"Sure," Cole answered.

"Now just grab one of them."

Cole grabbed one of the wires.

"Feel anything?" asked his partner.

"Not a thing," answered Cole.

"Good!" said Edney. "Don't touch the other one or you'll drop dead!"

———

LOUISIANA NEWS ITEM

Bayou. Kidnappers grabbed a little boy and two days later sent him home with a ransom note.

His parents immediately sent the kid back with the money.

———

Allen Klein, the famed San Francisco funny fellow, savors this snippet of satire:

Braxton and Hollis had jobs at a California cotton mill. One morning the foreman came along and found Braxton reading a letter to his coworker.

"Hey," cried the foreman, "what kind a horseplay you two guys up to?"

"Hollis got a letter from his girlfriend," explained Braxton, "but he can't read; so Ah'm readin' the letter for him."

"How come you got the cotton in your ears?"

"Hollis don't want me to hear what his girlfriend writ to him!"

Two Tennessee teenagers, Joey Bob and Jimmy Lee—on a bicycle-built-for-two—had a tough time getting up a steep hill.

"Ah didn't think we'd ever make it to the top!" said Joey Bob.

"Yeah," said Jimmy Lee, "and it's a good thing Ah kept the brakes on the whole time, or we'd a rolled right back down!"

———

Did you hear about the country boy who was so dumb he thought a Castro convertible was a Cuban bisexual?

———

Elliott Wolf, the Santa Rosa investment wizard, wows friends with this waggish dash of whimsy:

A San Francisco motorist following a taillight in a dense fog crashed into the car ahead of him when it stopped suddenly.

"Why didn't you let me know you were going to stop?" he yelled into the mist.

"Why should I?" came a voice out of the fog. "I'm in my own garage!"

Duayne met Patricia Ann from Birmingham at a Tuscaloosa ballroom. They danced every dance together. When the evening was over, he asked if he could see her next time he was in town.

"Yes," replied Patricia Ann shyly.

The young man hurriedly took out his pad and pencil and asked, "What's your number?"

"CApitol 4-6173."

After a long embarrassed pause, Duayne asked, "How do yew make a capital 4?"

———————

Jelks was arrested for rape. "Don't you worry none," said the sheriff. "You'll be treated fair. We'll make sure you have a lineup with un-uniformed policemen."

The sheriff was true to his word. The victim was brought in and lined up with some cops.

"Yep!" Jelks nodded. "That's her all right!"

———————

When Big Bubba ordered a pizza, the man at the counter asked him, "You want it cut into four or eight pieces?"

"Better make it four," said Bubba. "I'd never be able to eat eight!"

Did you hear about the country boy who took a book out of the library called *How to Hug,* only to discover it was Volume Ten of the *Encyclopedia Brittanica?*

————

Dilmer, six-foot-three, two hundred eighty pounds, was thrown from his seat when the Southern Railway train he was riding derailed. The giant teenager flew a dozen feet through the air before hitting headfirst against a steel partition. For a moment Dilmer lay dazed, rubbing his head. The conductor came by and kneeled down beside him.

"Don't move!" said the conductor. "We've called an ambulance."

"Naw," said the boy, getting to his feet. "I ain't hurt so bad. That steel wall musta broke my fall!"

————

Personnel Director: What would you do if you broke your arm in two places?
Vanderkron: I wouldn't go to them places no more!

Middle-aged Payton and Grimes were sitting in a cocktail lounge discussing their past lives.

"I've lived a good life," said Payton. "There's only one thing I'm ashamed of. My mother caught me once doin' something real embarrassing."

"Don't worry about it," soothed his friend. "All us kids did that."

"I know," said Payton. "But it was only yesterday that she caught me!"

————

A vacationing veterinarian was watching a bunch of fishermen catch tuna. He stopped a passerby and asked, "Isn't it wonderful how they can squeeze those two-hundred-pound fish into such little cans?"

————

Young Clyde took his girl out driving in the country. He parked the car in a lover's lane but just sat there. In a few minutes she decided to make the first move.

"Would yaw'l like to see where Ah had my operation?" she asked.

"No! I hate hospitals," answered the boy.

Jasper and Newton were walking through the outskirts of town when they spotted a human head lying in the road. Jasper picked the head up and held it high in the air to see it better.

"Golly!" he cried, "it looks like J.D. Bibb!"

"Naw!" said his buddy. "Ole J.D. was a much shorter guy!"

————

Did you hear about the dimwit who was so dumb he thought Gatorade was welfare for crocodiles?

————

Rigby drove into the city with his girl to catch their first play at a theater. Rigby rushed up to the box office and said, "Gimme two tickets for tonight's show."

"Sorry," said the box office attendant. "There are no seats left. We have only two standing rooms left."

"Well, I'll be hog tied! Only two left in standing room!" said the farm boy. "Are they together?"

Two Virginia boys, Sonny and Rick, went out hunting and split up. Sonny heard some rustling in the bushes and, by mistake, shot his friend. After trying to remove the bullet, he carried Rick to a doctor.

Two hours later, after the physician had patched up the wounded hunter, Sonny asked, "Please, Doc. How's my friend?"

"Well," answered the M.D., "he'd be a lot better off if you hadn't taken out his gut!"

––––––

First Hunter: I'll bet you can't shoot that rabbit!
Second Hunter: What makes you think I won't hit him?
First Hunter: Your gun isn't loaded.
Second Hunter: So what? That rabbit don't know it!

––––––

Perkin and Knolls, two Philadelphia lawyers, went hunting in North Dakota and killed a deer. They each grabbed a hind leg and began pulling it toward the truck. But the antlers kept dragging and slowing them down.

Another hunter passed by and said, "Why don't you pull that thing by the horns?!" And the men did.

Two hours later, Perkin said, "This is a good idea, Knolls. It's a hell of a lot easier than the way we was doin' it."

"Yeah," said his buddy. "But we keep gettin' further and further from the truck!"

"Can you read Chinese?"

"Yes, but only when it's printed in English."

———

Did you hear about the auto mechanic who went to a psychiatrist and insisted on laying under the couch?

———

Enoch and Arleigh had been out duck hunting since four in the morning and only had one duck.

"We're sure lousy duck hunters," said Enoch. "Let's go home."

"Nah!" appealed Arleigh. "Let's try a little longer."

"Something must be wrong," said Enoch. "Maybe we ain't throwin' the dogs up high enough!"

———

Tyfus applied for a job in a factory. The company doctor who was giving him a physical asked, "Have your eyes ever been checked?"

"No," said the worker. "They've always been brown."

"Why did your boyfriend return his Christmas tie?"
"He said it was too tight."

———————

"All right, you think you're so smart, why did God create man?"
"He couldn't teach gorillas how to mow the lawn."

———————

Private Skinner of the Foreign Legion hadn't seen a woman in years.

"I'm getting pretty frustrated," said the soldier to his sergeant. "What am I going to do?"

"See that camel over there?" answered the NCO. "The men are supposed to take that animal when they need to relieve themselves."

That night the sergeant was awakened by the camel's screeching and squealing. He discovered Skinner kissing and hugging the animal and having a great time.

"What're you doing?!" shouted the sergeant. "You were supposed to take the camel to where the women are!"

Hatton: I ain't as dumb as I look!
Folsom: You couldn't be!

————

Collins and Marley, two retired Rotarians, were out in a rowboat fishing. Suddenly, Collins landed a big one and remarked to his friend, "This is some place to fish! How we gonna remember where it is for next time?"

His friend thought for a minute and then jumped overboard, disappearing beneath the surface.

In a moment he climbed back on board.

"What'd you do?" Collins asked.

"I painted an *X* on the bottom of the boat so we can remember the spot!"

"Boy, are you stupid!" Collins berated his friend. "What'll we do next time if we don't get the same boat?!"

————

Tubbs was a contestant on a television quiz show.

"For ten thousand dollars," said the M.C., "tell us the meaning of Easter."

Tubbs thought for a moment and said: "This man comes out of the ground—"

"That's it!" shouted the M.C. "You've just won ten thousand dollars!"

"—and turns around," finished Tubbs. "And if'n he sees his shadow . . ."

Rundell and Tipton were working their first day in a coal mine. Rundell turned on his headlamp and said to his coworker, "I bet you five bucks you can't climb all the way up that beam of light."

"Oh, yes, I could," answered Tipton.

"For five bucks, I say you can't."

"Five bucks says I can!"

"Okay, then. Go ahead and climb it!"

"I'm no dummy," said Tipton. "I'd get halfway up and you'd turn the damn thing off!"

————

Did you hear about the rookie Rhode Island cop who gave out twenty-two parking tickets before he found out he was at a drive-in movie?

————

Chaffee could talk on any subject whether he knew anything about it or not. Mostly he didn't. One day his neighbor Nibley could stand no more.

"Do you realize," asked Nibley, "that you and I know all there is to be known?"

"Do you really think so?" said Chaffee. "How do you figure that?"

"Easy," answered Nibley. "You know everything except that you're a damn idiot. And I know that!"

How many Navy pilots does it take to change a light bulb?

Three. Two to tell you everything's okay and one to screw it in the faucet.

———————

Chuck: I keep seeing spots before my eyes.
Rusty: Have you seen a doctor?
Chuck: No, just spots.

———————

Wyatt, Milford and Calhoun were standing one on top of the other trying to measure a flag pole.

A man passing by yelled up to them, "Why don't you guys just take down the pole, lay it down on the ground and measure it?"

"We don't wanna measure the length, mister!" Wyatt sneered. "We wanna measure the height!"

Shingles were loose on Pennock's roof, and he complained about leaks to Barton, his neighbor.

"Why don't you mend the roof?" asked Barton.

"I can't today," Pennock replied. "It's pouring rain."

"Well, why don't you patch it in dry weather."

"It don't leak then!"

————

Hoot: How the hell can ya be so stupid?

Jessie: Well, it ain't somethin' yew can pick up overnight.

————

Snyder came home and found his house on fire. He rushed next door, telephoned the fire department and shouted, "Hurry over here! My house is on fire!"

"Okay," replied the fire chief. "How do we get there?"

"That's up to you," yelled Snyder. "Don't you still have those big red trucks?"

Benson had been found after being stranded on a desert island for five years. When he got off the plane at O'Hare airport, a beautiful blonde walked up to him and said, "How'd you like to have something you haven't had in years?"

"Don't tell me!" Benson lit up. "You've got filter cigarettes!"

———

Holton sat down in a Green Bay restaurant and said to the waitress, "Do you know whether the milk from this dairy is pasteurized?"

"Sure is!" she answered. "Every morning they turn the cows out to pasture."

———

Did you hear about the dimwit who went to visit his girlfriend and found she didn't have very much on?

He went back nine months later and she had a little moron.

Remember: If you want to make an accountant laugh tomorrow, tell him a joke today.

————

An army sergeant told Private Perkins to go to the end of the line. He did, but then returned.

"I thought I told you to go to the end of the line," barked the NCO. "Why did you come back?"

"Because there's already somebody there!"

————

Veronica was practicing the piano when suddenly there was a loud pounding on the front door. She opened it and found a breathless cop.

"What's the matter?!" she asked.

"Where's the body?!" demanded the officer.

"What are you talking about?"

"We just got a tip that some guy named Mozart was being murdered in this house."

————

What has eight legs and an IQ of forty?

Four guys watching a baseball game.

Henderson bought a new car and, after he left the showroom, decided to catch a movie. When he came out, Henderson noticed he'd locked the car and left the keys in the ignition.

He telephoned the dealer. "Which is the cheapest window to break?" he asked.

"You don't have to break any of the windows," explained the dealer. "I'll come right down with another key and we can open it together."

"No, no!" shouted the new car owner. "I gotta know now! It's about to rain and I wanna put the top up!"

Collegiate Chowderheads

Why do University of Arkansas graduates tape their diplomas to the windshields of their cars?

So they can park in handicapped spaces.

––––––

How do you keep an Oklahoma State student busy for a month?

Give him a package of M & M's and tell him to alphabetize them.

––––––

How do you know a Brigham Young student's been mowing the lawn?

The welcome mat is destroyed.

Professor Granger addressed his class: "If there are any dumbbells in the room, please stand up."

After a long pause, a lone freshman stood.

"And why do you consider yourself a dumbbell?" asked the professor.

"Well, I don't, sir. But I hate to see you standing all by yourself."

———

What does the *N* on the Nebraska football helmet stand for?

"Nowledge."

———

Tipton and Baldwin shared a room on the North Carolina campus. One day Tipton came in and said to his roommate, "I hear there's a new case of herpes in the dorm."

"Great!" said Baldwin. "I was getting tired of 7-Up!"

———

Why does a Texas Aggie keep his fly open?

In case he has to count to eleven.

Why did the University of Oklahoma researcher stay awake every night?

He was trying to find a cure for insomnia.

————

"You there in the back of the room!" shouted the instructor. "What was the date of the signing of the Magna Carta?"

"I dunno," was the reply.

"You don't know? Well, when was the Third Crusade?"

"I dunno," the victim replied again.

"I made this assignment last Friday. What were you doing last night?"

"I was out at a party with some friends. Didn't get home 'til five A.M."

"And you have the audacity to stand there and tell me that?! Just how do you expect to pass this course?"

"I dunno, mister. I was just told to come an' fix the radiator."

————

Why don't Purdue athletes eat pickles?

They can't get their heads in the jar.

The physics professor turned from the blackboard and said to his class, "I defy you to name anything faster than the speed of light."

"Just one thing," said the pretty coed. "A frat man on his way home after seeing a porno movie."

————

NEWEST DRINK AT NEW MEXICO STATE
Perrier and Club Soda.

————

Professor Dumbarton conducted an experiment at a small California agricultural college to show how a frog reacts to a human stimulus. The scientist explained: "At first the frog jumped sixteen feet. When I cut off one leg, I established that a three-legged frog could only jump twelve feet. Then I cut off another leg and yelled, 'Jump!' I concluded that a two-legged frog could only jump nine feet."

"I then discovered that a frog with one leg can jump only six feet. I cut off the last leg and shouted, 'Jump!' again, but the frog didn't move. I therefore concluded that a frog with no legs is deaf!"

What do you get when you cross a Texas Aggie with an ape?

A retarded ape.

———

Professor: Heavens! Someone stole my wallet!
Wife: Didn't you feel a hand in your pocket?
Professor: Yes, but I thought it was mine!

———

In the municipal offices of a New England city, there was a rule that only Harvard graduates could be promoted above a certain level. The last three college men to assume responsible jobs with the administration bungled their efforts badly. Their departments were a total mess.

This sign finally appeared just over the toilet paper dispenser in the city hall's men's room: HARVARD UNIVERSITY DIPLOMAS: TAKE ONE.

Three students from Michigan State, the University of Kentucky and Texas A & M on summer vacation in France were caught smuggling cocaine and sentenced to death by guillotine. The judge turned to the boy from Michigan and asked, "Do you have any final words, son?"

"Yeah, drop dead!" snapped the Wolverine.

Hearing this, the judge signaled for the sentence to be carried out. The executioner pulled the lever, and as the crowd gaped in astonishment, the giant blade came to a screeching halt three inches from the victim's throat.

"It's God's will! Let him go!" cried the judge.

Next the fella from U. of Kentucky was put on the block, and the judge asked again, "And what are your final remarks, my boy?"

"Go to hell!" shouted the student, and the judge signaled. The razor-sharp blade fell and miraculously stopped just a quarter inch from the condemned boy's neck. "It's the will of God!" exclaimed the judge. "Set him free!"

Finally the Texan was put into position. "Before you're beheaded," said the judge, "do you have any last words?"

"Yeh!" replied the Aggie. "If y'all will just put a little more grease on them grooves, the blade'll come down a whole lot easier!"

———

Did you hear about the Louisiana Tech professor who stood in front of a mirror for two hours, wondering where he'd seen himself before?

Professor: A wise man doubts everything. Only a pin-head is positive.
Student: Are you sure of that, sir?
Professor: Positive.

———————

"Professor, I hear your wife has had twins. Boys or girls?"
"Well, I believe one is a girl and one is a boy—but it may be the other way around."

———————

Professor Pollen went into the men's room on the train and found it crowded with other men.
When he came out ten minutes later, his wife said, "Darling, you've still got whiskers. Why didn't you shave?"
"Oh, dear! I thought I did," he said. "But there were six of us using the same mirror, so I must have shaved the guy standing next to me!"

———————

Astronomy Professor: What causes a half-moon?
Gwendolyn: When you can't get your jeans over your thighs.

What is the second stupidest thing in the world?

An Arkansas architectural student out in the middle of the ocean trying to build a foundation for a house.

What is the stupidest thing in the world?

An Arkansas contractor trying to build a house on the foundation.

Did you hear about the Western Kentucky professor who kissed the door goodbye and slammed his wife as he went by?

And then there was the UCLA professor who opened up his vest, pulled out his tie and wet his pants.

Housekeeper: Professor, there's a bill collector at the door. I told him you were out. But he wouldn't believe me.
Professor: No? Then I suppose I'll have to go and tell him myself.

Layne Littlepage, the talented young novelist, chortles lots over this lovable lampoon:

"Where's the car?" asked Professor Delbert's wife when he got home.

"Did I take it out?"

"Yes, you drove it to school this morning."

"I suppose you're right, my dear. I remember now that after I got out, I turned to thank the man who gave me a lift and wondered where he'd gone."

———

"Where are my shoes?" asked the Iowa State professor as the class ended.

"They're on your feet," said one of the students.

"So they are," said the professor. "It's a good thing you saw them, or I would have gone home without them!"

———

Higginbote and Goldstein, Fordham freshmen, were discussing what kind of work would supply them with big bucks after graduation.

"Well, I've always thought I'd like to be a doctor," said Higginbote. "Specialize in something or other. Like obstetrics, maybe."

"Obstetrics?" scoffed Goldstein. "At the rate science is going, you'd no sooner learn all about it when bingo!—somebody'd find a cure for it."

How do you measure a Villanova graduate's I.Q.?

With a tire gauge.

––––––

Kyle and Emmitt, two University of Miami students, were strolling along Miami Beach during spring break. Suddenly a seagull flying overhead dropped a load. It hit Kyle right in the eye.

"I'll go get some toilet paper," offered Emmett.

"Don't bother," said Kyle, "He's probably already miles away by now!"

––––––

Jamie decided to try out for the Ohio State baseball team. He arrived at the practice field carrying his glove and spikes.

The coach approached him and said, "Okay, Jamie. Name yer best playin' position."

"Sorta stooped over like this," answered the country boy.

Did you hear about the Penn State professor who went around in a revolving door for six hours because he couldn't remember whether he was going in or coming out?

———

Then there was the girl who, against her family's wishes, ran off and married a Princeton physics professor. The eloping bride received the following telegram from her parents:

"Do not come home and all will be forgiven."

———

Professor: I forgot to take my umbrella this morning.
Wife: When did you first miss it, dear?
Professor: When I reached up to close it—after the rain had stopped.

———

How many Wake Forest fraternity brothers does it take to make chocolate chip cookies?

Seventeen. One to do it and sixteen to shell the M&M's.

How do you get a Texas Tech senior's eyes to sparkle?

Shine a flashlight in his ears.

————

What do you call ten Utah State law students standing ear to ear?

A wind tunnel.

————

Dinkin, an Ohio farm boy, was trying to join a fraternity at the University of Alaska, but the boys didn't want him. They told him that in order to be accepted he'd have to do three things: drink a gallon of homemade liquor, wrestle a grizzly bear and make love to an Eskimo woman.

Dinkin guzzled down the booze and then staggered off into the woods. He returned the next day, his clothes tattered and torn.

"What happened?!" asked the frat men.

"Never mind!" said the boy. "Now where's that Eskimo woman you wanted me to wrestle?"

Why did the Oregon State psychology major climb up the chain link fence?

To see what was on the other side.

———

A Mississippi professor was at a party and became indignant when asked if college professors were absent-minded.

"Professors haven't got bad memories," he declared. "They're not absent-minded. Don't you think I know where I am right now, and don't you think tomorrow I'll know where I was last night? Would somebody like to ask me another question?"

"Yes," said another guest. "Is it true that professors are absent-minded and have bad memories?"

"Good!" said the professor. "I knew sooner or later somebody would ask me that question."

———

Biddle and Payne, two elderly English professors, were having lunch in the cafeteria.

During the course of the conversation, Biddle said, "A student gave me a peculiar answer in class today. I asked who wrote the *Merchant of Venice* and a sophomore said, "Please, sir, it wasn't me!"

"Ha, ha!" laughed Payne. "And I suppose the little snot had done it all along!"

Why are Georgetown graduates like Coke bottles?

They're both empty from the neck up.

————

Did you hear about the Duke science major who tried to blow up his instructor's car?

He burned his lips trying.

————

What is a Furman freshman doing when he grasps at thin air?

Collecting his thoughts.

————

"Did you hear? Lamont's gettin' a Ph.D."
"What does Ph.D. stand for?"
"In his case, Pin-headed Dope."

Tad answered the Tennessee State frat house phone. "Hi," said the voice, "this is Rollie. Come on over, we're having a real wildass party."

"Shit, Ah'd shore love to," said Tad, "but Ah got me a bad case of gonorrhea."

"Bring it along!" answered Rollie. "The way thangs is goin', mah buddies'll drink anythin'!"

————

Mrs. McKenzie was showing Corbett, the contractor, through the second floor of her new house to show him what colors to paint the rooms. "I'd like the bathroom done in white!"

Corbett walked over to the window and shouted, "Green up! Green up!"

"I want the bedroom in blue!" continued the woman.

The contractor listened and yelled out the window, "Green up! Green up!"

"The halls should be done in beige!" she instructed. Again, the man barked out the window, "Green up! Green up!"

"Will you stop that?!" shouted the woman. "Every time I give you a color, all you do is shout 'Green up!' What the devil does that mean?"

"I'm real sorry, ma'am!" explained Corbett. "But I got three Oklahoma basketball players down there tryin' to put in the front lawn!"

Did you hear about the UCLA track star who won a gold medal?

He was so proud of it that he had it bronzed.

———————

A survey was being taken on the University of Arizona campus. The survey taker asked a soccer player, "What do you think of bilingualism?"

"Oh, I think it's okay," said the boy, "if it's between consenting adults."

———————

Jim Tunney, the distinguished National Football League referee, delights audiences at his motivational programs with this joyful tidbit of jocularity:

Soderling, the star college halfback, was taking a math exam. The coach desperately needed him to play in the Syracuse game on Saturday, so the professor agreed to give him an oral exam.

"All right," said the prof. "How many degrees are there in a circle?"

"Uh, depends," said the boy. "How big is that there circle?"

Dwayne showed up at the practice field to try out for the Kansas State football team.

"What position do you wanna play?" asked the coach.

"Quarterback!" answered Dwayne.

The coach handed him a football and said, "Do you think you can pass this ball?"

"Hell!" said the boy. "If'n I can swallow it, I know I can pass it!"

———

How many Buckeye football players does it take to change a lightbulb?

One. But he gets three hours credit.

———

Caleb came from a small town in west Texas and was real thrilled when he made the A & M football team. One Monday afternoon the coach noticed his socks were filthy.

"Hey you featherbrain," said the coach. "You gotta put on a clean pair of socks each day before we go out for practice!"

By Friday, Caleb couldn't get his shoes on.

Did you hear about the Tennessee State student who went on a hunting trip?

He saw a sign along the road that read, "BEAR LEFT," So he got scared and went home.

————

Jeb and Eudell, University of Michigan athletes, were driving from Ann Arbor to Cleveland. Just outside the city limits they saw a sign: "CLEAN REST ROOMS." By the time they got to Cleveland, they'd cleaned 147 johns.

————

Two Kentucky psychology majors were walking through the campus. "Do you consider a 144 I.Q. high?"
"Yes!"
"For the whole basketball team?"

————

Arvil was coming out of the Texas University student building when he was stopped by two coeds.
"Would you like to become a Jehovah's Witness?" asked one of the girls.
"No, I really couldn't. I didn't see the accident."

How can you tell a Minnesota hockey fan?

Ask him what color the blue line is and wait. It may take him ten minutes to answer.

————

After an examination, the school doctor said to McQuade, "I'm afraid you've got VD. Any idea where you contracted it?"

"Yes, sir. It was during a wet dream!"

————

What do they call a bunch of Mississippi football players standing in a circle holding hands?

A dope ring.

————

How does a New York University psychology major turn on his lights in the morning?

By opening the car door.

What do you call a Carnegie Tech coed with half a brain?

Gifted.

————

All the fraternity brothers left the house for a long weekend—except for Grady, who decided to stay behind and get some studying done.

One night Grady heard a noise under his bed.

Fearing it might be a burglar, he leaned over and whispered, "Anybody there?"

"No," said the burglar.

"That's funny," the boy said to himself. "I could have sworn I heard a noise!"

————

Did you hear about the University of Miami fullback who stayed up all night studying for his urine test?

Then there was the Florida State defensive tackle who thought Hertz Van Rentals was a famous Dutch painter.

What did the University of Florida freshman say when his date blew in his ear?

"Thanks for the refill."

———

How can you tell if a California State coed is a good cook?

She can get the pop tart out of the toaster in one piece.

———

McKean, a North Dakota rancher, got rich even though he didn't have an education. Despite his success, he stayed unsophisticated and prudish.

On his deathbed, he said to Father Dempsey, "I'm leavin' half my fortune to the Church and the other half to the state college."

"It's the devil's work!" cried the priest. "That college takes decent boys and girls and makes them matriculate together. They even have the same curriculum!"

McKean cancelled the bequest to the college.

Redneck Bubbaheads

The phone in Rigby's Georgia farmhouse rang one evening. When he answered, the operator said, "This is long distance from Chicago."

"Ah knowed it's a long distance from Chicago!" answered the farmer. "How cum yew called to tell me that?"

———

Melburn was strolling along downtown Natchez with a framed picture under his arm.

"Hey, what yew got there?" asked a neighbor.

"Ah dunno much 'bout art," replied the redneck, "but Ah just bought me an original Michelangelo for two hundred dollars! It's one of the few he ever did in ballpoint!"

What does X X X stand for?

Three rednecks cosigning a note.

———————

Did you hear about the Oklahoma redneck who married an American Indian? They had a baby and wanted to name it to reflect both races.

So they called it Running Dummy.

———————

"Ain't that just dumb to put shoe polish in collapsible tubes?" said Terrell.

"Why?" asked his brother.

"Yew can't fool anyone that way," said the redneck. "Ah know'd the difference the minute Ah got the stuff in my mouth!"

Marley stopped at the town barbershop for a haircut. After thirty-five minutes of snipping and cutting, the barber held a mirror behind Marley's head. "How you like it?" asked the barber.

"Real fine," said the redneck. "But how 'bout makin' it jes a little longer in the back?"

———

IRS Agent: What's all this?
Bracken: Well, yew told me to bring all my records with me and Ah did. Here's some by Willie Nelson, Tammy Wynette, and Garth Brooks . . .

———

Sauer and Tolbert went to the zoo and watched in awe as a lion let loose with a spine-tingling roar.

"Let's get out of here!" said Sauer.

"Go on, if'n you want to," said the other redneck. "But Ah'm stayin' for the whole movie!"

Jett was tryin' to light a match. He struck the first one and it didn't work, so he threw it away.

He struck the second match. That didn't work either, so he tossed it.

Jett struck the third one and it lit up. "That's a good one!" said the redneck, blowing it out. "Ah'm gonna save it!"

————

Elmore walked into his favorite truck stop cafe and said to the owner, "Hey, Roy, you wanna take a chance on a raffle?"

"Whada ya win?"

"A million dollars!" said the redneck. "You get a dollar a year for a million years."

"How much are they each?"

"Ten cents. Two for a quarter. Or three for half a dollar!"

Moody was awakened by the telephone at four A.M. It was his Ku Klux Klan buddy, Crumm, calling long distance from Montgomery.

"What's the matter?" asked Moody. "Yew in trouble?"

"Naw!" said Crumm.

"Watch yew want, then?"

"Nothin'!"

"Then how cum yer callin' me in the middle of the night?" asked Moody.

"Cause!" said the other redneck, "the rates is cheaper!"

———————

Did you hear about the redneck who went to the doctor to get a hernia transplant?

Slaydon was standing in the middle of a hotel lobby without any clothes on when a policeman grabbed him.

"Okay, fella!" said the cop. "Let's get something to cover you up and go down to the station!"

"Wait a minute!" Slaydon said, resisting.

"Listen, mister!" protested the cop. "You can't just stand around here stark naked!"

"But officer," begged the redneck. "Ah'm waitin' for mah girlfriend. We wuz up in the room and she said, 'Honey, let's get undressed and go to town.' Ah guess Ah just beat her downstairs!"

———

How can you tell which kid in the first grade class is the son of a redneck?

He's the one with the rusty zipper and the yellow sneakers.

———

For several months Birch had been collecting unemployment checks. When they stopped he decided to become a mailman and went down to take the civil service exam.

The first question was, "How far is the earth from the moon?"

"Look," said the redneck to the examiner, "if'n that's gonna be mah route—yew can forget it!"

Kelso met Hensley on the street. "Hey!" said Kelso, "how cum Ah never hear from yew? Why don't yew call me on the tellyphone?"

"Yew ain't got no tellyphone!" said Hensley.

"Ah know," said Kelso. "But yew do!"

————

INTELLECTUAL REDNECK
A guy who doesn't move his lips
when he reads.

————

Dewey and Odell met on the Brownsville main street. "Say," said Dewey, "Ah hurd yew and yore wife is goin' ta night school ta take Spanish lessons. How cum?"

"Uh huh," answered Odell. "We went and adopted us a little Mexican baby, and we wanna be able ta understand him when he gets old enough ta talk!"

Eulus stood in front of the take-out window of a Rawlins fast food restaurant. "I want two hamburgers," he said. "One with onions, and one without."

Redneck counter man: "Okay. Which one's without the onions?"

———————

Barbour and Romayne were on a jet to Cincinnati when the captain's voice came over the loud speaker: "We've lost an engine, but there's no cause for worry. We have plenty of power left. But," added the pilot, "we will be a little late."

A few minutes later another engine went out, and the captain repeated the same message.

Soon the third engine conked out, and the captain made the announcement again.

"Piss!" said Barbour. "If'n that last engine goes out, we could be up here all night!"

For a weddin' present Ledbetter gave his son Amos two hundred dollars. Two weeks later he asked him, "W'atcha do with the money, son?"

"Ah bought me a wristwatch, Pappy!" answered the boy.

"Yew dumb ignoramous!" yelled his father. "Yew should 'av bought yoreself a rifle!"

"A rifle? What fer?"

"Suppos'n one day yew cum home and find some guy sleepin' wid yore wife," explained the older redneck. "W'atcha gonna do? Wake him up and ask him what time it is?"

Thetchel lived in a tiny Alabama town and couldn't get a job. So the town council decided to hire him to keep the Civil War cannon polished.

The young redneck did a good job and kept the brass polished and the cannon shining.

One day Thetchel went to the mayor's office and told him he was quitting.

"Why, son?" asked the mayor.

"Ah've been savin' money to buy mah own cannon. Ah'm goin' in ta business for mahself!"

Did you hear about the redneck who planted Cheerios in his backyard?

He thought they were donut seeds.

———

Grubbs stood in front of the judge in the courtroom. The judge asked, "Now, tell me. Why did you park your pickup where you did?"

"Whaal, Yer Honur. There was this sign there that sayd, 'Fine for Parking.' "

———

INSIDE DOPE
A redneck who hasn't been born yet.

———

Jeb's teacher asked him the difference between his own age and his brother's age.

"Mah mama tol' me last year that mah brother was one year older than me," answered the boy. "So, accordin' to mah calculations, this year we both must be the same age!"

Cole was walking down the road when he ran into Hoskins. "Howdy, Cole!" said Hoskins. "How's everythin' up yore way?"

Cole shook his head. "Not real good," he replied. "Mah daughter's took down with the typhoid, and the ol' woman's dyin' of pneumonia. Ah shore got a peck o' trouble!"

"Ah'm mighty sorry," said Hoskins. "Ah don't know nothin' 'bout typhoid fever, and there ain't no pneumonia in our family neither. When it comes to pecker trouble, though, Ah sure can sympathize with ya!"

———

Sheridan and Wyman were passing the time down at the general store. "Hey!" said Sheridan, "Ah just read that it took that Eye-talian Michelangelo more'n twenty years to finish the dome of the Sistine Chapel!"

"That right?" said Wyman. "The dumb bunny! He could a done it a lot faster if he got him one o' them paint rollers!"

———

When a small Montana village decided to buy a new fire truck, the town council met to decide what to do with the old one. Randall, an old rancher, stood up. "Ah think we should keep the old truck," he said. "We can use it for all them false alarms!"

Izzard went into a Baltimore bank to cash his check. Since he didn't have an account there, the teller asked if he could identify himself.

"Sure," said Izzard. "There a mirror around here?"

"There's one on the wall right beside you," said the clerk.

Izzard took a glance in the mirror and heaved a sigh of relief.

"Yep!" he said. "It's me, all right!"

———

Mayne and Willard, two hillbillies, were in a rowboat on a lake fishing. Suddenly the spray from a motorboat racing by flooded their boat.

"How we gonna get the water out?" asked Mayne.

"Easy," said Willard. "We just bore a hole in the bottom of the boat and let the water drain out."

The men drilled a hole in the bottom, and more water started rushing in.

"Wait a minute!" exclaimed Mayne. "We need another hole so's the water comin' in through the first one has a place to go back into the lake!"

Young Vestal was walking in his Florida backyard when an alligator bit him.

"Mama!" yelled the boy. "A gator jus' bit off mah foot!"

"Which one?" called his mother from inside the cabin.

"How the hell should Ah know?!" he shrieked. "They all look alike to me!"

————

What's even smarter than a smart redneck?

A dumb hillbilly.

————

Faxon and Elgin, two hard hats on a construction job, watched in amazement as their coworker, Larvel, performed some rather unusual antics. He kept tapping himself upward on the elbow.

"What the hell's he doing?" asked Faxon.

"He's goosing himself," replied Elgin.

"On the elbow?"

"Sure." The other hard hat grinned. "You know that rednecks don't know their ass from their elbow."

"Sally Mae, marry me," said Murl, "and after our weddin' night yew'll swear Ah had me a transplant from a mule."

Sally Mae did, and the next morning she said, "Yew were right about the transplant. Ah wonder what that animal's doin' without his brain."

————

Slim walked into his local post office and noticed a new sign on the wall:

MAN WANTED FOR ROBBERY
IN MONTANA

"Gosh!" he said, "If'n only that job was in Texas, Ah'd take it!"

————

Hoss and Slick were passin' the time swigging Dr. Peppers and playing dominoes.

"Did yew know Jesse James was a champion weight lifter?" Hoss asked his friend.

"Ah don't believe it!" said Slick.

"It's true!" said Hoss. "Ah heerd he held up two ten-ton trains—one after the other!"

Zack and Tybe, two Alabama farm boys, bought themselves a truckload of watermelons for a buck apiece.

They sold each one for a dollar. After counting up their cash, they realized they'd wound up with the same amount of money they'd started out with.

"See!" said Tybe. "Ah told yew we shoulda got a bigger truck!"

————

"Mah son's real smart!" crowed the redneck mother to an acquaintance. "He's only six but he can already spell his name backwards and forwards!"

"What's his name?" asked the friend.

"Bob."

————

A Nebraska teacher met the mother of one of her pupils in the supermarket.

"Ah hate to tell you this," said the schoolmarm, "but yore son is illiterate."

"That ain't so!" his mother replied angrily. "His father 'n me was married a whole year befor'n he was born!"

Ruby Alice walked up to the desk of a Bowling Green motel and signed the register with the letter "O."

"Why'd you put that circle down?" asked the clerk.

"Cause Ah can't write," replied the girl.

"Why don't you sign with an 'X'?" asked the man.

"Ah used to," she answered. "But when Ah got me a divorce, Ah took back mah maiden name!"

————

Culley was rushed to the emergency room of a Columbus hospital. The doctor on duty was shocked to discover that he had scalded his testicles.

"How did this happen?" asked the physician.

"Ah was makin' me some tea," replied the redneck, "an' the directions said, 'Soak bag in hot water'!"

————

Pickney sat before the personnel manager in an Oregon lumber mill.

"Ah was born in Alabama," said the redneck, hoping to land a job.

"What part?" asked the manager.

"All of me, of course!"

Did you hear about the redneck farmer who was so stupid his wife had to stamp This Side Up on her stomach?

————

The July temperature in Joplin climbed over the one hundred mark. Despite the scorching heat, Bozell was outside painting his house.

A passerby stopped for a moment to watch him and then asked, "How cum yer wearin' two jackets?"

" 'Cause," said the redneck, "the directions on the can say ta put on two coats!"

————

Harkins had just joined the police when he was assigned to duty at a south Florida nudist camp. That night he reported back to the precinct house.

"Well," asked the Sergeant, "how's it goin'?"

"Real good!" replied the redneck. " 'Cept'n this here badge is killin' me!"

Kennen was having a drink in a saloon when his neighbor, Stakely, came rushing in. "Ah think somebody's stealin' yore pickup truck!" the man said breathlessly.

Kennan ran outside, but came back right away.

"Well, did yew stop him?" asked Stakely.

"Naw!" said the redneck. "He was too fast. But Ah got his license plate before he got away!"

———

Did you hear about the Nebraska redneck who filled out an employment application?

In the blank labeled "Church Preference" he filled in: Red brick.

———

What do they call the stork that delivers redneck babies?

A dope peddler.

Billy Bob and Jed were having a few Michelobs in a bar. Billy Bob was reading his *National Enquirer.*

"Says here 'we only use a third of our brains'!" he read aloud.

Half an hour later Jed turned to his friend and said, "Ah wonder—what we do with the other third?"

———

Roach and Tubbs, two Tennessee laborers, were working on a State Highway project.

"Hey!" shouted Roach to his friend. "Stop throwin' that dirt out a the ditch!"

"Ah hav' ta throw the dirt somewhere," said Tubbs.

"Yew blockhead!" yelled Roach. "Dig yoreself another hole and put it in there!"

———

What do you get if you cross a retarded West Virginian with a baboon?

A redneck intellectual.

During a break on a North Dakota office building project, one of the construction workers approached Pyle.

"Ah heard the boys is gonna strike," he said.

"What fer?" asked Pyle.

"Shorter hours."

"Good fer them!" said the redneck. "Ah always did think sixty minutes was too long fer an hour!"

————

Why did the redneck drive his pickup truck over the side of the cliff?

He wanted to try out his new air brakes.

————

ELEVEN O'CLOCK NEWS BULLETIN

One of the television networks is currently creating a special series to be aired every Monday night in prime time. The show will be two hours long and feature a redneck trying to count to one hundred.

Cloyd went to a Charleston dentist complaining his gums had shriveled up and his teeth were falling out.

After examining him, the dentist said, "Your mouth is really bad. Do you brush?"

"Ah sure do!" replied Cloyd. "Everee single day!"

"What do you brush with?" asked the dentist.

"Preparation H," said the redneck.

———

Interviewer: How do you spell Mississippi?
Redneck: Which one? The river or the state?

———

Did you hear about the redneck who was buried in a lake?

His son drowned trying to dig his grave.

———

"Why do rednecks act like such morons?"
"Who says they're acting?"

Down in Florida, a Philadelphian, a Bostonian and a Raleigh redneck completed the police academy course and were close to becoming cops.

"Just one more question," said the police chief to the candidate from Philadelphia. "Who killed Jesus Christ?"

"They used to say it was the Jews," said the Philadelphian, "but they proved that wrong."

"Good!" responded the chief. "You can start work Monday."

He then called in the former Bostonian.

"Who killed Jesus Christ?" the cop asked the candidate.

"The Romans," answered the man from Massachusetts.

"Okay. You can begin duty Monday morning."

Finally he called in the redneck.

"Who killed Jesus Christ?" asked the top cop.

"Waal, Chief, that's kind of a hard question. Ah'd like to think on it overnight and tell yew my answer in the mornin'."

The chief agreed. When the redneck got home his wife asked, "Well, did you get the job?"

"Shore did!" he answered. "And Ah'm already on mah first assignment—a big murder case!"

Married Meatheads

"I had to marry you to find out how stupid you are," said Emmaline to her husband.

"You should have known that the minute I asked you," he replied.

———

A married couple was having a big fight over breakfast. The husband said, "I never thought it was possible for one woman to be so beautiful and yet so stupid."

"It's God's will," she answered. "He made me beautiful so I'd be attractive to you. He made me stupid so you'd be attractive to me."

———

Wife: Would you sooner lose your life, or your money?
Husband: My life, of course. I'll need my money for retirement.

Kelp and his wife were sitting at the dining table having their nightly squabble.

"Mister!" she shouted, "you're so dumb you think Barnum and Bailey are married to each other!"

"What difference does it make," he replied, "as long as they're in love?"

————

"Sheep are such stupid animals. Don't you agree, Elizabeth?"

"Yes, my lamb."

————

Did you hear about the young Long Island couple who got married, and the bridegroom went to Albany alone for the honeymoon?

The bride had already been to the capital.

The Ainsleys had never ridden on a train. Twenty minutes after they left the station Mrs. Ainsley said to her husband, "The conductor told me that this train'll soon go under a river."

"Well, don't just sit there!" he cried. "Close the window!"

————

Bad weather had forced the Chicago airport to close, and Metcalf decided to go home by train. His wife met him at the station. "You look exhausted," she noted.

"Been riding backwards for ten hours," he explained. "I never could stand that."

"Why," said his spouse, "didn't you ask the person sitting opposite to change seats with you?"

"I couldn't do that," said Metcalf. "There wasn't anybody there."

————

Bobbi Jean had been married only three days. She walked into a Tulsa drug store and asked for a bottle of men's deodorant.

"The ball type?" asked the clerk.

"No," she replied. "Fer under his arms."

Edgar and his new wife had a huge fight, so he decided to fix dinner that night.

"This meat don't taste too good," said his spouse.

"I can't imagine why," he replied. "I burnt it a little, but I put sunburn oil on it right away."

————

There was a severe epidemic in town, so the doctor, in true medical tradition, worked around the clock by converting his kitchen into a temporary office. But the crowds pouring into the place soon made it inadequate. "Some of you will have to be vaccinated in the basement," he said.

The mayor stood up and protested, "Doctor, I want to be vaccinated in the arm or not at all!"

————

The Grahams were riding on a scenic tour train for the first time. They brought bananas for lunch. Just as the husband bit into his banana, the train entered a tunnel. "Did you take a bite of your banana?" he asked his wife.

"No."

"Well, don't!" exclaimed Graham. "I did, and I went blind."

Randy and J.J. were having a beer in the local watering hole when they suddenly heard a loud burst of laughter.

"What're those guys laughing at," asked Randy.

"Hank Cantrell. He's about the dumbest guy in town. Got married so many times, he just married one of his former wives again and didn't even know it."

"Boy, that is dumb!"

"And he never would have found it out except that he recognized his mother-in-law!"

————

Rosalie was visiting her bandaged husband in the hospital. On the way out, she said to the nurse, "My husband always says, 'Why should I be the first to dim my headlights?' "

————

Wife: Why are you so upset?

Husband: The garage charged me fifty dollars for towing my car a mile. I got my money's worth, though. I kept my brakes on!

Did you hear about the Arkansas addlebrain who had a vasectomy so he'd stop having grandchildren?

———

No matter how many mistakes Mayfield made, he somehow always managed to place the blame on his wife.

One morning she stared at him and snapped, "Did you ever take time to think if you've got a brain?"

"Certainly not," he retorted. "Such a thing would never enter my head."

———

Sharron Fell, the renowned Monterey reflexologist, makes clients chuckle with this cutie:

Mr. and Mrs. Bromwell were sitting in the living room watching television.

"Say," said the woman, "do you think Julia Roberts is her real name?"

Her husband thought for a minute and then replied, "Do I think whose real name is Julia Roberts?"

Nils Shapiro, California's masterful media magnate, breaks up buddies with this beaut:

Harry and his wife were watching an old Clint Eastwood western on TV. As Clint rode through a pass, Harry's spouse said, "I'll bet you a dollar his horse steps in a gopher hole and falls!"

"Okay," said Harry. "You're on!"

Sure enough, the horse stumbled. After the bet was paid, the wife said, "I ought to tell you, I saw the movie before. That's how I knew."

"So did I," said Harry, "but I didn't think a horse would be dumb enough to fall in the same hole twice!"

————

Husband: I've lost quite a lot of weight.
Wife: I don't see it.
Husband: Of course you don't. I've lost it!

————

"I hate to say it, honey, but this toast is really tough."
"You're eating the paper plate, darling!"

Pritchard walked into his Pensacola living room flashing a large, shiny pinkie ring.

"That's some diamond you got there," said his wife. "Is it real?"

"If'n it ain't," said Pritchard, "I been cheated out of five bucks!"

————

Did you hear about the Brooklyn cab driver whose wife had triplets and he went out looking for the other two guys?

————

The father-to-be was nervously pacing up and down the hospital corridors. Finally, the nurse stopped him.

"Congratulations," she said. "You have twins."

"Wonderful," said the new father, "but please don't tell my wife—I want to surprise her."

————

Randall finished taking a shower and said to his wife, "It's too damn hot today to wear any clothes. What do you think all our neighbors would say if I mowed the lawn in the nude?"

"Probably that I married you for your money."

Mark Oman, the genteel Golfaholics Guru, gets guffaws on the links with this gleeful pinch of mirth:

"Where did you get those new golf clubs?" asked Mrs. Cranby.

"Don't worry, darlin'. They didn't cost a thing," answered her spouse. "They were marked down from six hundred dollars to three hundred dollars. So, I bought them with the three hundred bucks I saved!"

———

"Hello, is this the fire department?"

"Yes, sir, can we help you?"

"Could you please tell me where the nearest fire box is? I want to report a fire!"

———

When Warner came home from work his wife greeted him excitedly. "You better speak to Junior about swearing. I overheard him using terrible language on the way home from school this afternoon."

"What!" shouted Warner. "I'll teach him to swear!"

He scrambled up the stairs and, on the top step, stumbled over Junior's skates. He tumbled back down and came to a painful stop.

"That's enough for one lesson!" said Mrs. Warner.

"Sorry I'm late, dear," said Brewster, "there's water in the carburetor."

"Where is the car?" asked his wife.

"In the lake."

———————

Two Texas ranchers, Joe Ed and his neighbor Billy Ray, were taking an afternoon ride through the foothills.

"Ole buddy," moaned Joe Ed, "have Ah got me an absentminded milkman."

"Watch yew mean?" asked Billy Ray.

"Well, mah wife's been feelin' kind of poorly these past couple a days, so Ah stayed home today and took care of her. Early this mornin' there was a knock on the door and Ah went to answer it. Ah was nekkid, so Ah threw on mah wife's bathrobe."

"So?"

"When Ah opened the door that danged fool of a milkman grabbed holt a me, started rubbin' mah ass and then gimme a big kiss. Ah reckon his wife must have the same color bathrobe as Ellie Jo!"

Monroe, a Massachusetts shoe manufacturer, made a lot of money on the stock market and decided to have his entire house redecorated. Despite his wife's protests, he insisted on handling everything.

One day when the stained glass windows were delivered, he shouted at the contractor, "You take those right out and have all the stains removed!"

———

Dudger got an out-of-town construction job and asked his pal, Polson, to check up on his wife to see that she didn't fool around with anybody.

Six months later Dudger returned and found his spouse and his best friend in bed doing the very thing he'd tried to avoid. Dudger called his wife every name in the book and then threatened divorce.

"And as for you, you dirty dog!" he shouted at Polson. "Couldn't you at least stop while I'm talking to you?!"

———

Bernstein rushed into his Bronx apartment and shouted to his wife, "Hey, honey! Guess what?"

"What?"

"I just bought four new tires. What a bargain."

"What a dimwit! Leave it to you to buy tires when you don't even own a car."

"Yeah? Do I say anything when you buy a bra?"

Fernell and his wife were taking their first cruise down to the Caribbean.

At breakfast the next morning she asked him, "Did you hand over my jewels to the ship's purser for safe-keeping like I told you?"

"I didn't have to, darlin'," he replied, "there was a lovely little wall safe in the cabin called a porthole."

———

"Hey, dummy!" said Chadwell to his wife. "Close the window, it's cold outside."

(Closing window) "There! Now it's warm outside."

———

Orpha Mae: Bobby Joe, I want yew to go 'round to the minister and arrange for having the baby christened.
Bobby Joe: You mean to say you gonna let somebody hit that little thing over the head with a bottle?

When Lucinda returned from her honeymoon she telephoned the doctor. "Those birth control pills you gave me aren't working!"

"What do you mean, not working?" asked the surprised physician. "I just gave them to you a week ago!"

"Well," replied the newlywed, "they keep falling out!"

————

Bridegroom to the hotel clerk: "How much do we owe for the room?"

"Thirty bucks apiece."

Johnson figured for a minute and handed him a hundred and fifty dollars.

————

Emmett had just described his vacation experiences to a friend.

"Sounds as if you had a great time in Texas," he said. "But didn't you tell me you were planning to visit Colorado?"

"Well," Emmett replied, "we changed our plans because, uh . . ."

His wife cut in, "Oh, tell him the truth, Em. It's ridiculous. Emmett simply will not ask directions!"

"I came home yesterday an' found some stranger makin' love to my wife," said Louie.

"What'd you do?" asked his friend.

"I fixed that sucker. I threw his umbrella out the window and prayed for rain."

———

Electrician: Your doorbell doesn't work, mister, because you have a short circuit in the wiring.

Husband: Well, dammit, then lengthen it!

———

Rankin got into the Montana mine elevator, chuckling out loud.

"What's the joke?" asked the foreman.

"I sure have a big laugh on Kelly," replied Rankin. "I just found out he paid my wife twenty bucks to kiss her, and I do it for nothing!"

———

Rocky and Pete were on a break at the construction site.

"I come home last night and I find some strange guy kissing my wife," said Rocky.

"Holy smoke! What'd you do?" asked Pete.

"Ha! I fixed them! I shut off the lights so they couldn't see what they was doin'!"

Sal and Frank were in the Wrigley Field bleachers having a few brews, watching the Cubs.

"My new next door neighbor must think I'm in the coast guard," mused Sal.

"Why's that?" asked Frank.

"Every time I answer the phone he keeps askin', 'Is the coast clear?' "

————

Young Chapman was wheeling a baby carriage around the block on a very hot afternoon.

"Honey!" shouted Mrs. Chapman from an upper window of their house.

"Lemme alone!" he called back. "We're all right."

An hour later his wife pleaded once again, "Honey!"

"Well, what do you want?" he replied. "Something wrong in the house?"

"No, honey, but you've been wheeling Melissa's doll all afternoon. Isn't it time for the baby to have a turn?"

————

Festus said to his wife, "Weleta, now tomorrow why don't you take Junior to the zoo?"

"What do yew mean, take him?" answered his wife. "If they want him, they kin come and git him!"

Husband: This match won't light.
Wife: What's the matter with it?
Husband: I don't know—it lit before.

———

Mrs. Brown shook her husband awake.

"Will you help me straighten up the house?" she asked.

"Why?" her husband replied. "Is it tilted?"

———

"You are beyond a dimwit!" screamed Mrs. Watson at her husband. "You are illiterate."

"Is that so? Well, the joke's on you. My parents were married."

———

Velma May and her friend, Cora Sue, were having an afternoon coffee klatch.

"Oh, shoot!" said Velma May. "Look out the window. Here comes mah husband with a dozen carnations."

"Golly," said Cora Sue. "What's wrong with a bunch of carnations?"

"Yew kiddin'! Mah legs'll be spread apart all weekend now."

"Gee whiz, honey," said Cora Sue, "ain't yew got a vase?"

Parrish was taking the state civil service exam.

"Have you ever committed sodomy?" asked the psychiatrist.

"No, sir," he said. "One wife's enough for me!"

———

Kramer came home and found his wife in bed with another man. He took a gun out of the drawer and put it to his own head. The wife's lover jumped up and shouted, "Hey! What're you doing!"

"Shut up!" yelled Kramer. "You're next!"

———

Clete, a young farm boy, and Lila Mae, his new wife, came home from their ten-day Las Vegas honeymoon. The next evening the bridegroom, wanting to show off his newly discovered sophistication, volunteered to fix cocktails before their dinner.

Clete was out in the kitchen for a long time when his spouse came in and inquired, "Wot's taking you so long?"

"Ah rinsed the ice cubes in this here hot water," he replied, "and now Ah can't find 'em!"

A Detroit dentist and his wife were in a motel. In the middle of the night a man crashed into their room and, at gunpoint, forced the husband out of bed.

He drew a circle on the floor with a piece of chalk and then said, "Stand in that circle. If you move out of it, I'll kill you!"

The intruder hopped in bed with the dentist's wife, made love to her for over an hour and then left. "My God!" cried the distraught woman. "Why didn't you do something?!"

"I did!" responded the dentist. "I jumped out of the circle three times!"

———

"I got a terrible toothache, Virgil. It's killin' me. Do you know a good dentist?"

"You don't need a dentist. I had me a real bad toothache yesterday, but my wife put her arms around me and kissed me and cuddled me and loved me up and in no time the pain went away. You oughta try the same thing."

"Great idea. You're a real buddy. Where can I find your wife?"

Guthrie was complaining to his wife that their neighbor kept sneaking up on him and slapping him on the chest and breaking the cigars in his pocket.

"But," said Guthrie, "Ah figured out a way to teach him a lesson."

"Watch yew gonna do?" asked Mrs. Guthrie.

"Ah'm gonna fix him!" said her husband. "The next time he slaps me on the chest, Ah'm gonna have me three sticks a dynamite in mah pocket!"

————

Kristi went to Dr. Gibson, a psychiatrist, seeking help about her love life. The shrink warned her that he could help only if she was open and honest with him.

"Tell me," said Gibson, "have you ever looked into your husband's face while making love?"

"Yes."

"Okay," said the analyst. "When you looked into your husband's face while you were making love, what emotion did you see there?"

"I saw great anger," replied Kristi.

"And," said the doctor, "when you saw this great anger, what was your husband doing at the time?"

"He was on a stepladder, looking at me through the bedroom window . . ."

Parental Pinheads

"Son, you sure do ask a lot of questions," said the father. "I'd like to know what would have happened if I'd asked as many questions when I was a boy."

"Perhaps," said the boy, "you'd've been able to answer some of mine."

————

At dinner, Seth said to his father, "Dad, I got into trouble at school today and it's all your fault."

"How's that?" asked the master of the house.

"Remember I asked you how much $500,000 was?"

"Yeah, I remember."

"Well, 'a helluva lot' ain't the right answer."

————

Tad looked up from the book on ancient history he was reading and asked his father, "Pop, what's a millennium?"

"Well," he muttered, "I think it's something like a centennial, only it has more legs!"

"Dad," said Rickey, "what is electricity?"

"Uh," replied his father, "I don't really know too much about electricity."

A few minutes later the boy said, "How does gas make the engine go?"

"Son, I'm afraid I don't know much about motors."

"Dad," said the boy, "what is anthropology?"

"Anthropology?" The father frowned. "I really don't know."

"Gee, Dad, I guess I'm making a nuisance of myself."

"Not at all, son. If you don't ask questions, you'll never learn anything."

———

"How is your daughter's marriage working out?"

"Fine. Of course, she can't stand her husband—but then there's always something, isn't there?"

"Honey," said Mrs. Beldon to her husband, "Lester's teacher says he ought to have an encyclopedia."

"Encyclopedia, my eye!" exclaimed Beldon. "Let him walk to school like I did."

————

Talbot and his son James were called to Mrs. Crenshaw's classroom.

"Mr. Talbot," said the teacher, "I asked James 'Who shot Abraham Lincoln?' and he said that he didn't do it!"

"Well, teacher," said Talbot, "if my kid said he didn't do it—he didn't do it!"

Father and son left the school, and on their way home Talbot turned to the boy and asked, "Tell me, son, did you do it?"

————

Son: Where are the Himalayas?
Father: If you'd put things away, you'd know where to find them.

"What are you reading?" demanded the father of his seven-year-old.

"A story about a cow jumping over the moon," was the reply.

"Throw that book away at once," he commanded. "How many times have I told you you're too young to read science fiction?"

————

Down at the office Bostwick boasted to one of his buddies, "My son Arthur is smarter even than Abraham Lincoln. Arthur could recite the Gettysburg Address when he was ten years old. Lincoln didn't say it till he was fifty!"

————

"Can I go outside and watch the solar eclipse?" asked Rupert.

"Okay," replied his father, "but don't stand too close."

An irate father stormed into the principal's office. "I demand to know," he screamed, "why my son Winslow was given a zero on his English examination."

"Now, don't get excited," said the principal. "We'll get your Winslow's English teacher in here. I'm sure she has some explanation."

A few minutes later, the English teacher arrived.

"Why did you give Winslow a zero on his English final?" demanded the father.

"I had no choice," said the schoolmarm. "He handed in a blank paper with absolutely nothing on it."

"That's no excuse," shouted the father. "You could have at least given him an 'A' for neatness!"

————

Father: Don't you think our son gets his brains from me?
Mother: Probably, dear. I still have all of mine.

————

Mrs. Filmore returned home from a business trip and asked her husband, "How did Greg do on his history exam?"

"Oh, not so good," he replied. "But it wasn't his fault. They asked him about things that happened before he was born!"

Nicole returned from the supermarket and was met at the door by her husband. "I'm so proud of our little son," he said excitedly. "Do you know what he was doin' just now?"

"No, what?" asked Nicole.

"Why, he was standin' in front of the mirror with his eyes closed so he could see what he looks like when he's asleep!"

———

"Hey, Pop," pleaded Angelo, "can I go to the zoo to see the monkeys?"

"What's the matter with you?" asked his father. "Why would you wanna go see the monkeys when your Aunt Marie is here?"

———

Paul Brocchini, the peerless Pacific Coast real estate agent, loves this snippet of drollery:

Miles returned to his posh Beverly Hills home from college one hot afternoon and decided to cool off with a dip in the family pool.

"Wait a minute, son," announced his father, "you can't go in the pool with long hair!"

"What?" exclaimed Miles.

"You heard me! It's unhealthy. Get a haircut and you can go in!"

"But, Dad!" said the young man. "Some of history's greatest men had long hair."

"Those are the rules."

"Moses had long hair, Dad," protested the son.

"Well," said the father thoughtfully. "Moses can't swim in our pool either."

Young Bobby was being fitted for glasses, and his father, standing beside him, said, "Now, remember, son. Don't wear them when you're not looking at anything."

———

"Papa, who was Hamlet?"

"You birdbrain! Bring me the Bible and I'll show you who he was."

———

Mobley's eyes were glued to the television set when his son tapped him on the shoulder. "Dad, will you help me find the least common denominator?"

"Haven't they found it yet? They were looking for that when I was a kid."

———

"Dad, do you believe in Buddha?"

"Why, of course, but I think margarine is just as good."

"Dad, why do you write so slow?" asked Dennis.

"I have to," replied his father. "I'm a slow reader."

— — — —

Mrs. Ellis came home from work one evening to find her three-year-old son lighting up a cigar. She raced into the kitchen where her husband was making dinner.

"Hey!" she announced. "This is terrible! I just caught Matthew lighting a cigar!"

"You put a stop to that right now," he shouted. "That kid is altogether too young to be playing with matches!"

— — — —

Whalen: I hate to tell you this, Mr. Reed, but your son's a moron!

Reed: What! Where is that young good-for-nothing? I'll teach him to join a fraternity without consulting me!

— — — —

Doting Mother: I'm so proud of Genevieve. She's taking both Algebra and French! Genevieve, darling, say Good morning in Algebra for Mrs. Sizemore.

Bentley and his wife and son were sitting at the dinner table when the boy suddenly blurted out, "Gee, you're dumb, Mom. You don't know anything."

"Now, son," scolded Bentley, "you musn't be picky about your mother's little faults."

————

"My son's a kleptomaniac."

"That's wonderful! Where is his office?"

————

"Grandpa, why don't you drink tea anymore?"

"I don't like it ever since that tea bag got stuck in my throat."

————

During a flood in a small Ohio town, a young girl was perched on top of a house with a little boy.

As they sat watching articles float along with the water, they noticed a baseball cap float by. Suddenly, the cap turned and came back, then turned around and went downstream. After it had gone some distance, it turned again and came back.

"Do you see that baseball cap?" said the girl. "First it goes downstream, then turns around and comes back."

"Oh, that's my dad," replied the boy. "This morning he said that come hell or high water, he was going to cut the grass today."

"I gotta 'A' in spelling," Tony told his father.

"You dope!" he replied. "There isn't any 'A' in 'spelling'!"

————

Did you hear about the dumb father who returned from lunch and saw a sign on his door, "Back in 30 minutes," so he sat down to wait for himself?

————

Son: What is an autobiography?
Father: Er, the story of an automobile.

————

Haskell rushed down to the Atlantic City beach where his daughter had just been rescued from drowning.

"Mister," said the handsome lifeguard, "I've just resuscitated her!"

"Okay then," said the father, "you're just going to have to marry her!"

Old-fashioned Zachary approached Lureen's father, intent upon asking him for her hand in marriage.

"Sir," he blurted out, "I have an attachment for your daughter, and—"

"See here, young man," interrupted the parent, "when my daughter needs accessories, I'll buy them myself."

———

"Luke, how does yore daughter like bein' newly hitched to that soldier boy?"

"Real fine. Just this morning she wrote to the army for his favorite recipes."

Blake and his parents were drinking at the bar in a train station when they heard a whistle. The three of them rushed out of the bar onto the platform only to discover that they had missed the train.

"The next train is in one hour," said the stationmaster.

The three went back into the bar. The parents had another drink; Blake had a Pepsi.

Again they heard a whistle, rushed out and discovered the train pulling away.

"Next one is sixty minutes from now!" said the stationmaster.

An hour later, Blake, with his mom and dad, raced out onto the platform, and his parents leaped onto the train as it pulled away. The boy was left standing on the platform and began to laugh uproariously.

"Your parents just left you," said the stationmaster. "Why are you laughing?"

"They came to see me off!"

National
Knuckleheads

What is the most common educational degree in New Mexico?

Kindergarten dropout.

———

Why do New Mexicans drink less Kool-Aid than folks in other states?

Because they have such a hard time getting two quarts of water into that little envelope.

———

How do you recognize a Virginian staying in a fancy hotel?

He's the one trying to slam the revolving door.

Did you hear about the Baton Rouge bride who cancelled the wedding when she heard her friends were planning to give her a shower?

————

A Bangor resident went to the airport and asked for a roundtrip ticket. The ticket agent asked, "Where to?" The Mainer said, "Well, back here, of course."

————

Why is Otto the most common name in Minnesota?

There's only two letters to remember.

————

Kowalski and Janzek left Hamtramack and went out in the woods looking for Christmas trees. They looked all day without any luck. Near nightfall Kowalski finally said, "Janzek, I'm takin' the next tree we come to, whether it has lights on it or not!"

Loralee sat opposite a man on a desolate train ride through West Virginia. He looked terribly sad and lonely, but in a while he said, "Excuse me, miss! Would you like to take a look at my *Cosmopolitan?*"

"Mista!" said the hillbilly girl. "If'n yew dare try, ah'll scream!"

––––––

How did the Cleveland cop lose his contact lens?

The putty fell out of his eye!

––––––

The South Carolina couple planned to get married and went to the doctor for their blood test. The M.D. then tried to explain to them about sex. The boy just listened with a dumb expression on his face.

So the doctor took his fiancée over to the examination table, had her lie down and then made love to her.

"Now do you understand?" asked the physician.

"Yeah," said the boy. "But how often do I have to bring her in?"

Did you hear about the Georgia accountant who absconded with all the accounts payable?

———

OHIO NEWS ITEM

A Toledo man was admitted to the city hospital last night with severe burns after dunking for French fries at a Halloween party.

———

"They caught Hughie last night burglarizin' a house in Birmingham 'cause he broke two windows."

"Why'd he do that?"

"One to get in, and one to get out."

———

What can most Alabama kids do by the age of twelve?

Wave bye-bye.

———

How can you tell when a North Dakotan has class?

When the words on his tattoo are spelled correctly.

Calvert was complaining to his South Dakota neighbor, Jeffcoe, that his house was being overrun with rats.

"Here's what you do," suggested Jeffcoe. "Just pour boiling water into their holes."

Three days later they met again.

"That was a good idea of yours," said Calvert, "but I can't find nobody to hold the rats."

———

Swint and Fess, two Oklahoma cowboys, were resting their horses out on the range.

"What'd Emmaline give yew for yore birthday?" asked Swint.

"Pair of cufflinks," said Fess. "But I ain't got no use for them. I can't even find anyplace to get my wrists pierced."

———

An insurance salesman was getting nowhere in his efforts to sell a policy to an Abilene rancher.

"Look at it this way," he said. "How would your wife carry on if you should die?"

"Well," answered the Texan, "I don't reckon that's any concern of mine, so long as she behaves herself while I'm alive."

Did you hear about the Omaha mother who got tired of putting name tags on her son's shirts, so she had his name legally changed to "Machine Washable"?

————

The teacher asked a Louisiana teenager to count to five. The youngster proceeded to count to five on his fingers.

Then the teacher asked, "Can you count any higher?"

The boy raised his hands over his head and counted to five again.

————

Ross Hersey, Virginia's favorite storyteller, regales crowds with this merry knee-slapper:

Two farmers met at the General Store.

"How is it your stock breed so good, and mine hardly breed at all?" one asked.

The other explained he was giving the animals special sex pills from the vet that made them crazy to mate.

"Sex pills? What's in them?"

"I don't know what's in 'em, but they taste like peppermints."

Jeremy Vernon, the consummate classy comedian, cracks up crowds with this joyful caper:

A Pittsburgh steel worker was driving through northern California's apple country.

He stopped at an orchard and asked the owner, "How much are yer apples?"

"All you can pick for one dollar," said the rancher.

"Okay," said the Pennsylvanian. "I'll take two dollars' worth."

————

Did you hear about the New Yorker who was killed in a pie-eating contest?

The cow sat on him.

————

At the Cedar Rapids Chamber of Commerce meeting the treasurer reported a deficit of two hundred dollars. One of the chamber members stood up and said, "I vote that we donate half of it to the Red Cross and then give the other fifty dollars to the Salvation Army."

What's considered a major cultural event with social significance in Idaho?

A black-and-white Road Runner cartoon.

————

"How come you're only watering half your lawn?" a perplexed tourist asked a Richmond resident.

"I just heard there was a fifty percent chance of rain."

————

What's considered a solid hour's reading in Iowa?

The back of a cereal box.

————

Four Independence boys, Pugh, Sumter, Kilby and Grayson, were walking down a Clay County road when they came to a high, solid brick wall. Wondering what was behind it, Pugh, Sumter and Kilby boosted Grayson so he could take a look.

"Looks like one of them nudist camps," reported Grayson.

"Men or women?" asked Pugh.

"Can't tell," said Grayson. "They don't have no clothes on."

A North Dakota farmer was visiting Las Vegas. He had no money to gamble, so he watched the games and bet mentally. In no time at all, he'd lost his mind.

———

A St. Louis mother telephoned the capitol building over in Jefferson City and asked to speak to the game warden. After being switched from office to office, a voice finally said, "Hello."

"Are you the game warden?" she asked.

"Yes."

"Finally Ah've got the right person!" she said. "Could yaw'l gimme some help with my son's birthday party?"

———

Did you hear about the Texan who moved to Oklahoma and raised the IQ level of both states?

———

How many South Dakotans does it take to go ice fishing?

Four. One to cut the hole in the ice, and three to push the boat through.

The night was dark when two men came up to the run-down cabin in the West Virginia hills and kicked the door. "Say, you all right, Orval?" they asked. "We found a body by the creek, and we kinda thought it might be you."

"What'd the fella look like?" asked Orval

"Sorta like you, Orval. A no-account."

"Have shoes on?"

"Yep."

"Overalls?"

"Yep."

"Shirt?"

"Yep."

"Was he shaved?"

"Seems like he were."

"Nope! 'Twarn't me, then!"

———

A woman walked into a South Carolina country store and said, "Do you keep brown sugar?"

"No, ma'am," replied the owner. "When it gets dirty we throw it away."

———

Iowa girl: Daddy, I'm pregnant.
Father: Are you sure it's yours?

If three guys, one from Ohio, one from Indiana and one from Kentucky—went skydiving together and none of the chutes opened, who would be the last one to hit the ground?

The guy from Kentucky, because he'd have to stop to get directions.

———

Why don't Nebraskans throw dinner parties?

They can't remember how to spell R.S.V.P.

———

What do they call anybody with an IQ of ninety in Louisiana?

Governor.

———

Did you hear about the Kentucky hillbilly who took his pregnant wife to a supermarket because he heard they had free delivery?

Then there was the hillbilly who asked his friends to give him their burnt-out light bulbs.

He wanted to start a dark room.

What's a henpecked Georgia husband?

A guy who doesn't know how to tell his pregnant wife he's sterile.

———

What do Mississippi mothers write on the labels of their kids' clothes?

"Shirt . . . Pants . . . Dress . . ."

———

A Hoosier, a Kentuckian and a West Virginian were on a Hollywood TV quiz show. The host asked them to complete the sentence: "Old MacDonald had a . . ."

The Indianan said, "Old MacDonald had a carburetor."

"Sorry," said the MC. "That's incorrect."

"Old MacDonald had a flat tire," said the Kentuckian.

"Wrong," said the host.

"Old MacDonald had a farm," said the West Virginian.

"That's correct!" shouted the MC. "Now—for $200,000, spell farm."

The West Virginian thought hard and then spelled carefully: "E-I-E-I-O."

Did you hear about the Montana moron who went looking for a gas leak with a safety match?

————

What are the rules of the famous Virginia Beach guessing game?

One player leaves the room, and the others have to guess which one of them has left.

————

Coleman moved to Wyoming and was sitting in the unemployment office applying for a job.

"Have you any experience in coal mining?" asked the clerk.

"Yeah, in Pennsylvania," he replied.

"They're using that new safety lamp down there now, aren't they?"

"Ah don't know, mister," said Coleman. "I worked on the day shift."

Why did the Minnesotan buy only one snow boot for winter?

He'd heard there was going to be only one foot of snow.

———

What are the worst five years in the life of a West Virginian?

Third grade.

———

What's the difference between a Kansan and Yogurt?

Yogurt has culture.

Doc Blakely, the lovable Texas tall-tale teller, gets howls on the speaking circuit with this generous gift of historical hilarity:

Early Texas governors were not very well educated. There was once a chief executive who thought "grammar" was his father's mother. On one occasion this governor went hunting and forgot his gun. He phoned his secretary and asked him to send the gun. "The phone connection's bad," said the secretary. "I couldn't catch that last word. Spell it."

The governor replied, " 'G' like in Jesus; 'U' like in onion; 'N' like in pneumonia—GUN, you damn fool!"

———

Did you hear about the Murfreesboro muddlebrain whose father told him about the birds and the bees?

The next day, the Tennessean was stung by a bee and thought he was pregnant.

———

Why do folks from Arkansas find it so hard to read?

Because they never learned to move their lips right.

How do Alaska CB radio operators say "10-4"?

"5-5-2-2."

———

What's the only thing thicker than a Kansan's sideburns?

What's between them.

———

Treadwell walked into a Biloxi stationery store and asked, "Have you got any invisible ink?"

"Certainly sir," said the owner. "What color?"

———

What's the most popular TV show in Billings?

"90 Minutes"—they have to slow it down so people can follow it.

———

A visitor from Indiana was running up and down the Las Vegas Strip sticking dimes into parking meters. "What are you doing?" asked a curious bystander.

The Hoosier replied, "I just love this outdoor gambling!"

Two tough-looking truckers from North Dakota stopped at a cafe outside of Great Falls. They were soon in a big argument with some local ranchers.

"If you guys want to tear each other apart," shouted the bartender, "go outside!"

The truckers left with the ranchers right behind them. In only five minutes the Montanans were back at the bar.

"What happened?" asked the bartender.

"Them dogs from North Dakota went an' pulled out their razors on us! But it turned out okay. They didn't have no place to plug 'em into!"

———

Mark Padow, the whimsical Washington wit, wins chuckles from colleagues with this wacky whippet of wordplay:

Polk and Bowen were driving along South Carolina Highway 21 when suddenly Polk pulled the pickup over to the side of the road.

"I don't think my turn signals is a workin'," he said to his buddy. "Go stand in back of the truck and tell me."

"Okay," said Bowen, getting out and walking to the rear of the vehicle. He stood silent for a while 'til the driver finally shouted, "What's happenin'?"

"They're workin' . . . they're not workin' . . . they're workin' . . . they're not workin' . . ."

Did you ever see a country boy in New York whistle for a cab?

He puts two fingers in his mouth and hollers, "Taxi!"

————

Titus was on a Knoxville elevator with several other people. As the elevator moved up, he stared at the small fan revolving slowly in the elevator ceiling.

"It's amazin'," he said to the other people, "that such a small fan could lift all these people!"

————

What's the first lesson a Staten Island teenager learns at driving school?

How to open a locked car with a coat hanger.

————

What does a Wisconsinite call his pet zebra?

"Spot."

What do you call a Georgian who works for the U.S. Forest Service?

An overachiever.

———

What do you get when you cross a flower with a Montana civil service worker?

A blooming idiot.

———

What's the easiest job in Florida?

Intelligence officer in the Florida National Guard.

———

Farmers Roach and Tubbs met on the main street of a small Utah town. After exchanging greetings Roach said, "Hey, brother, if you kin tell me how many chickens I got in this here sack, I'll give you both of them."

Tubbs paused for a moment, rubbing his chin and then proudly answered, "Three!"

"No fair, brother," said Roach. "You peeked in the sack!"

Did you hear about the Brooklyn bubblebrain who was two hours late for work because the escalator got stuck?

—————

Then there was the numskull New Jersey surgeon who finally had his hospital privileges taken away.

It wasn't so much all the patients he lost. It was the deep gashes he made in the operating table.

—————

Back in the Old West three Texas cowboys were about to be hung for cattle rustling. The lynch mob brought the three men to a tree right at the edge of the Rio Grande. The idea was that when each man had died, they'd cut the rope and he'd drop into the river and drift out of sight.

They put the first cowboy in the noose, but he was so sweaty and greasy he slipped out, fell in the river and swam to freedom.

They tied the noose around the second cowboy's head. He, too, oozed out of the rope, dropped into the river and got away.

As they dragged the third Texan to the scaffold, he resisted, "Please! Would yaw'l tighten that noose a little bit? I can't swim!"

Little Cora Mae answered the knock on the door of the farmhouse outside Huntsville. The caller asked to see her father.

"If yew've cum about the bull," she said, "he's fifty dollars. We got the papers an' everythin', and he's guaranteed."

"Young lady," said the man, "I want to see your father."

"If'n that's too much," said Cora Mae, "we got another bull for twenty-five dollars, and he's guaranteed, too. But he don't have papers."

"Look here!" repeated the man. "I want to see your father!"

"If'n that's too much," said the girl, "we got another bull for only ten dollars—but he ain't guaranteed."

"I'm not here for a bull," said the man angrily. "I want to talk to your father about your brother, Clovis. He's gotten my daughter into trouble!"

"Oh, I am sorry," said Cora Mae. "You do gotta see Pa 'bout that, 'cause I dunno what he charges for Clovis."

Foreign Fatheads

Why do Iraqi police officers walk in threes?

The first knows how to read, the second knows how to write and the third is to keep an eye on the two intellectuals.

———

Yazid and Ishkal, two Iraqi terrorists, were on their way to plant a bomb. On the way they had to drive up a very bumpy road.

"Go steady," said Yazid. "We don't want the bomb to explode."

"Stop worrying!" said Ishkal. "If it goes off, I've got a spare in the trunk."

———

Did you hear about the Iranian terrorist who switched off the fans of his stolen helicopter because he couldn't stand the draft?

Then there was the Albanian who planted lightbulbs in his garden.

He heard that tulips grew from bulbs.

———

And what about the East German race car driver at Indianapolis who had to make seventy-five pit stops?
Three for fuel.
Four to change the tires.
And sixty-eight to ask directions.

———

The Iraqis were offended by the vicious jokes told about them during the Gulf War. In defense, they were quick to remind friends about their soldiers' great bravery during the fierce fighting.
The Iraqis claim to have bare handedly thrown sticks of dynamite into the hordes of attacking Americans. The GI's caught the sticks of dynamite, lit them, and threw them back.

Why did they discontinue driver's education and sex education in Syria?

Because the camel died.

————

Al-Hassan sat in the office of Dr. Salih, a brilliant neurosurgeon skilled in transplanting human brains.

"You have several donor brains amongst which to choose," said the surgeon.

"What are they?" asked the Arab.

"You can have this Russian brain for only $50,000," said the doctor. "Or here's an American brain, which I can transplant for $100,000. But—if you can afford it—I recommend this adult Iraqi brain over here. It's $500,000."

"How can you possibly justify such a high price for an Iraqi brain?" asked Al-Hassan.

"Because it's never been used!"

————

Saddam Hussein waged a psychological warfare campaign during the Gulf War using a propaganda agent modeled after the famous "Tokyo Rose." He got "Baghdad Betty" to tell the American GIs: "While you're out here dying in our deserts, your wives are home making love to Tom Cruise, Kevin Costner and Bart Simpson."

What do you get when you cross a French Canadian with a monkey?

Nothing. A monkey's too smart to screw a French Canadian!

————

Pierre and Claude, two French Canadian postal workers, were chatting over lunch.

"How is your wife?" asked Pierre.

"She's in bed with laryngitis," replied Claude.

"Mon dieu!" said his friend. "Is that damned Greek around again?!"

————

Madames Flambeau and Traville, two Montreal housewives, met at a supermarket.

"I hear your husband had a postmortem operation," said Madame Flambeau.

"Yes," replied Madame Traville, "but not until after he was dead. If only they'd done it a bit earlier, it might have saved his life!"

Why are Canadians given only a half hour for lunch?

They don't want to have to retrain them.

———

Did you hear about the guy from Newfoundland who was twenty-two years old before he knew which part of the olive to throw away?

And then there was the Newfie who was found dead in his jail cell with twelve bumps on his head.
He'd tried to hang himself with a rubber band.

———

GROSS IGNORANCE
144 Newfies.

———

What's the difference between a Newfie and a pig?

One likes to eat, sleep, belch and roll in the mud. The other is considered intelligent and has a curly tail and a flat snout.

What's the difference between a Newfie and a chimpanzee?

One's hairy, smelly and picks his nose. The other can be taught to talk to humans.

———

Strindberg left Oslo and was met at the New York pier by his happy relatives.

"Welcome to America!" they all shouted.

After thanking them profusely for their kindness, Strindberg raised his hand to ask for silence.

He then proudly started to show off his knowledge of English by rattling off the months of the year: "Yoon, You-lie, All-guts, Split timer, Ox timber, no vonder, all vinter!"

———

Ole rushed down to the pier just as the ferry was pulling away. His friend, Lars, yelled from the boat. "C'mon, yump, Ole! Yump!"

"Aye can't make it!" cried Ole.

"Sure ya can!" called Lars. "Ya can make it in two yumps!"

Hedmann was driving one hundred miles an hour when he was stopped by a motorcycle cop.

"What's your hurry, buddy?" asked the officer.

"My brakes gave out," explained the Norwegian, "so I was trying to hurry home before I had an accident."

———————

John Kinde, the mirthful motivational magician, elevates audiences with his inspiring message and this merry mouthful:

A beat-up, disheveled Scandanavian was sitting in the gutter in front of a North Dakota saloon, laughing hilariously as the blood dripped from his nose.

"What's the joke?" asked a passerby.

"Aye bane in there at da bar an' a faller cum up to me and hit me in da eye and sayd, 'Take dat, you dam Norvegian!' An he poonch me on da nose and say, 'Dat for you, you dam Norvegian!' An he kick me into da street. Ha, ha!"

"But what's so funny about that?"

"Vy, can't you tell? Aye bane a Svede!"

———————

"Helga, tell me something. Why do Swedish men always have stupid grins on their faces?"

"Because they're stupid," said her friend.

Did you hear about the Norwegian orchestra that stopped in the middle of a performance to clean the saliva out of their instruments?

And it was a string orchestra.

———

Then there was the Danish hemophiliac who tried to cure himself with acupuncture.

———

And let us not forget the Finn who spent a fortune building a storm cellar in case there was an earthquake.

———

Sing Lee recently arrived from China and got lost in San Francisco. Frantically he telephoned his cousin to ask directions.

"Look up at sign and tell me where you are," said the relative.

He did and reported, "I on corner of Walk and Don't Walk."

Why does the Philippines ban rectal thermometers?

They cause too much brain damage.

———

Why are there so few skyjacking attempts by Mexicans?

What good is having a parachute if you can't count to ten?

———

What is long, brown and has a cumulative I.Q. of eighty?

A Cinco de Mayo parade.

———

Martinez gazed through the bars at the jailor.

"Can you read and write?" asked the jailor during the booking process.

"Write, not read," replied the prisoner.

"Write your name, then," the jailor instructed.

Martinez scrawled huge letters across the paper handed to him.

"What's that you wrote?" asked the warden.

"I don't know," replied the Mexican. "I told you, I can't read!"

Did you hear about the Mexican bricklayer who went crazy trying to lay a cornerstone in a roundhouse.

————

Dick Alexander, the terrific transatlantic travel writer, treats chums to this titter getter:

Buntington, a British newspaperman, got back to London after touring the U.S. for his paper. His fellow correspondents gathered around him one evening at the Press Club wanting to learn something about the recreation and amusement of Americans.

"Well," said Buntington, "Americans play a lot of strange games. There's one called 'Damn it.' "

"No! It couldn't be!" exclaimed a newsman.

"Yes, it's true. It's played in auditoriums. Hundreds of people fill the seats and have small numbered cards on their laps. A man on stage calls out a lot of numbers, and finally one person jumps up and shouts 'Bingo!' Then all the others exclaim, 'Damn it!' "

"Sir Charles," asked Lord Witherspoon. "Did you hear the joke about the Egyptian guide who showed some tourists the two skulls of Cleopatra—one as a girl and one as a woman?"

"No! Let's do hear it!" replied Sir Charles.

————

Sir Reginald was riding in a New York taxicab when the driver challenged him to solve a riddle.

"The person I'm thinking of has the same father as I do, and the same mother, but it's not my sister and it's not my brother. Who is it?"

The Britisher thought a moment and gave up.

"It's me!" said the driver, slapping his knee.

"By Jove! That's jolly good!" said the Brit. "I must try that on the chaps at the Club!"

A month later, Sir Reginald was sipping cognac with his cigar-smoking cronies when he remembered the joke. "Gentlemen," he said. "The individual I have in mind is not my brother, and not my sister, yet this person has the same parents that I do. Who is it?"

After several thoughtful minutes, all the members conceded defeat. "Who is it?" one begged. "Come on, Reggie! Give us the answer!"

Reggie slapped his knee in triumph: "It's a taxicab driver from New York City!"

Jim Poulos, Wyoming's gardening wizard, passes on this pinch of playfulness:

Kramanakis left Athens and immigrated to New York. He got a job through relatives who taught him to say "Apple pie and coffee" in English so he could order in a restaurant. The next day Kramanakis walked into a diner.

"What'll you have?" asked the waitress.

"Apple pie anna coffee," said the immigrant.

Since that was all he could say, he was forced to eat apple pie and coffee every day for a month. When he complained to his relatives, they taught him to say, "Ham sandwich."

Armed with the new addition to his vocabulary, Kramanakis told the waitress, "Ham sandwich."

"White or rye?" she asked.

"Apple pie anna coffee," replied the Greek.

———

Why is the computer center business in Puerto Rico such a miserable failure?

The night duty technicians always forget to stoke up the furnace.

———

Did you hear about the Puerto Rican secretary who was getting so experienced she could type twenty mistakes a minute?

Then there was the Puerto Rican surgeon who made medical history.

He performed the first appendix transplant.

————

Why did Rudolfo salute the box of Cornflakes in the supermarket?

Because the label said General Foods.

————

Rojas was visiting New York and ran into Felix on Broadway.

Rojas: Hey, man! When did you get here from San Juan?

Felix: Yesterday.

Rojas: How you come? Sea or air?

Felix: I dunno. My wife buy the ticket.

————

How does a Russian Aeroflot pilot navigate?

By reading street signs.

Ivanovich was stopped on a Moscow street by his friend. "Why you look so downhearted?"

"I can't understand it," he answered. "My neighbor took out two hundred thousand rubles' worth of life insurance and he died anyway."

Michelcheve walked up to an airport ticket counter and asked, "When is de next plane to Buffalo?"

"At five-thirty this afternoon," said the clerk. "But it's a local flight with stopovers in Washington and New York. The whole flight takes about four hours."

"That be too long," said the Russian.

"The best I can do is a direct flight the day after tomorrow," said the clerk.

"Okay. I wait for that one!"

A Siberian couple decided to start a chicken farm.

They bought two chickens, took them home, dug a hole in the backyard and buried the birds headfirst.

The next morning they got up excited, went to the garden and discovered the chickens were dead.

The Siberians discussed what had gone wrong over breakfast and decided to buy two more chickens. This time they planted them in the yard feet down.

The next morning, they got up excited, raced to the garden and found the birds had died.

The couple discussed what went wrong over breakfast and decided to write to the minister of agriculture explaining their problem.

Within a week they received a prompt reply. The letter read:

"Please send a soil sample."

Klinski and Dieslak were working on a building site when Klinski suddenly shouted, "Watch out! The bricks are falling off the wall!"

Just then, a brick fell and hit Dieslak, taking off his ear. He lay on the ground bleeding profusely.

"Take it easy," said Klinski. "I find your ear and take you to hospital. They soon sew it back on."

Klinski searched in the rubble, found Dieslak's ear and took it over to where he was lying on the ground.

"Okay," said the Russian. "I got it!"

Dieslak took one look at the ear and cried, "That's not mine, you dumbbell! My ear had a cigarette behind it!"

————

Santobal, a newly arrived Filipino immigrant, walked up to a traffic cop.

"Hey, Mr. Policeman!" he said. "Can you tell me right time?"

"Three o'clock," replied the officer.

"Damn!" said the Filipino. "What going on in this country? Every time I ask somebody for time I get different answer!"

Li Wu, walking down Broadway in New York on a dark night, passed by an alley. Two muggers jumped him, and though he put up a terrific fight, they got him down.

When they searched him they were amazed to find such a small amount of money in his pockets.

"You mean you put up a fight like that for a measly sixty-seven cents?" asked one of the muggers.

"Hell, no!" said the Chinese. "I thought you want the five hundred dollar in my shoe!"

———

Shen Yung decided that for a change he'd try eating something for dinner that wasn't Chinese. He went into Vito's Trattoria and ordered lasagna.

"Okay," said the waiter. "What would you like to have? Red wine or white wine?"

"It make no difference," said Shen Yung. "I color blind."

———

What do you call an Italian with a vasectomy?

A humanitarian.

Ralphie and Louisa were having their usual battle of the sexes.

"Italian men are all stupid," screamed Louisa.

"Oh, yeah?" yelled her husband. "I'll have you know it was an Italian man who invented the toilet seat!"

"And I'll have you know," said his wife, "it was an Italian woman who thought of putting a hole in it!"

————

Theresa and Angie, two computer technicians, were talking about their marriages over lunch.

"How long can a man live without a brain?" asked Theresa.

"Depends," said Angie. "How old's your husband?"

————

Carmella and Mario were out on their first date.

"Have you ever read Shakespeare?" asked Carmella.

"No," said Mario. "Who wrote it?"

Grandma Panzini had been voting in America for thirty years and finally decided to become a citizen. She arrived in court on the appointed day.

The first part of the test was on American history. The judge held up a picture of Abraham Lincoln and asked, "Who is this?"

"Dat's a Abraham Lincoln!" said the woman.

His Honor then held up a picture of George Washington. "And who is this?" he inquired.

"Datsa his wife!" said the grandma with pride.

————

BAGHDAD NEWS ITEM
Iraq has just ordered
two thousand septic tanks from Russia.
As soon as the Iraqis learn to drive them,
they are going to invade Iran.

————

Mrs. Ohito and Mrs. Fugiyama were waiting to be served at the fish market.

"How's your daughter Lisa doing?" asked Mrs. Ohito.

"Ah, she spend all her time with Socrates, Aristotle and a Plato," said Mrs. Fugiyama.

"Whatsa matter? She no like Japanese boys?"

The Filipino surgeon was scrubbing up after the operation. "So, Dr. Aquila, how did Mrs. Manita's appendectomy go?" asked an intern.

"Appendectomy?" shrieked Aquila. "I thought it was an autopsy!"

———

Why can't the Philippines field an ice hockey team?

The players all drowned in spring training.

———

How do Filipinos count money?

One-a, two-a, three-a, four-a, another-a . . .

———

What do Filipinos call Canada? Upper U.S.

What do Filipinos call Alaska? Way Upper U.S.

———

Venzetti walked into a Fifth Avenue bank. "S'cuza, I like-a to talk with the fella what arranges the loans."

"I'm sorry," replied the security guard. "The loan arranger is out to lunch."

"In dat-a case," said the Italian, "let me talk-a to Tonto!"

O'Ryan left Ireland to try his luck in the U.S. Getting on the ship he was stopped by an old woman. "I have a son in America," she said. "He lives in a little white house in Connecticut. I haven't heard from him in fifteen years. If you happen to meet him, please tell him to write to his poor old mother. His name is Dunn."

O'Ryan landed in New York. After a few months he took the bus up to Connecticut and told the driver, "Let me off at the little white house."

Thinking his passenger needed to relieve himself, the driver dropped him off at a park. O'Ryan spotted the attendant. "Could you be tellin' me where to find the little white house?"

Certain he meant the men's room, the attendant said, "Go straight down this lane and turn left." Thrilled that at last he'd find Dunn, O'Ryan followed the directions. Just as he got to the little white house, a man came out zipping his fly.

"You Dunn?" asked O'Ryan.

"Yeah," said the man.

"Then why don't you write to your poor old mother in Ireland?!"

Sweeney and Phelps were sitting in a Killarney pub discussing architecture.

"Modern buildings are far more beautiful than old ones," declared Sweeney.

"An' just try to show me one new building," countered Phelps, "that's lasted as long as the ancient ones!"

————

"Heat," explained Moynihan to his friend Fagan, "makes things expand, and cold makes them contract."

" 'Tis mad you are entirely!" said Fagan. "Whoever heard the like of that?"

"Well," replied Moynihan, "how else do you account for the days being longer in summer and shorter in winter?"

————

Quinn was sitting in a pub having a beer. A Welshman walked up to him and said, "Say, what's that big purple thing on your face?"

"It's a birthmark," replied Quinn.

"Yeah? How long have you had it?"

Muldoon and Nolan were relaxing in a Belfast park. "I hear you got a letter from your brother, Denny, that went to America," said Muldoon.

"Faith, an' I did that," replied Nolan.

"An' what did the boy say about hisself?"

"I can't tell you," said Muldoon. "On the outside of the envelope was printed RETURN IN FIVE DAYS, so I mailed it back to him."

————

An Englishman, a stranger to Dublin, was on a bus and asked Haggarty, the passenger beside him, if he was right for the town hall.

"Quite correct," said the Irishman. "This bus goes to the town hall. You get off at the stop before I do."

————

Did you hear about the Irishman who tried to swim the English channel?

Halfway across he decided he couldn't make it so he swam back.

And what about the Irishman who went out to his garden and put a floodlamp on his sundial?

He wanted to be able to tell the time at night.

————

Why are Irish jokes so simple?

So the English can understand them.

————

Mrs. Kerrigan and Mrs. Dooley were walking home together from church. "Me son Jimmy's comin' home tomorra!" said Mrs. Kerrigan.

"That's nice," replied Mrs. Dooley. "But I thought he was sent up fer five years."

"That's true," said her companion. "But he got time off fer good behavior."

"Oh, my!" said Mrs. Dooley. "It must be a blessin' to you to know you've got such a fine son!"

————

Doctor: That deafness cure help your brother?
Archie: Sure did! He hadn't heard a sound in years, and the very day after he took that medicine, he heard from America!

"What did Shawn like most about his trip to Paris?"

"He said it was lovely to hear the French pheasants singing the Mayonnaise."

———————

Mrs. O'Donovan herded her large family of twins into the cinema and began explaining to the cashier which of them should be entitled to half price.

"These two," said Mrs. O'Donovan, pointing to the first pair in line, "are under ten. These two are under eleven. These two are under twelve. These two are under thirteen. And the oldest twins at the end of the line won't be fourteen until next week."

"In the name of Saint Agnes, the virgin martyr!" said the dazed cashier. "Do you and your husband have twins every time?!"

"Not at all!" Mrs. O'Donovan blushed. "Lots and lots of times we don't have children at all!"

About the Author

This is Larry Wilde's 49th joke book, and with sales of over 12 million copies, it is the largest selling series of its kind in publishing history. The *New York Times* calls him "America's best-selling humorist."

He is also the author of *The Great Comedians Talk About Comedy* and *How The Great Comedy Writers Create Laughter,* both considered definitive works on comedy technique.

A former stand-up comedian, Larry Wilde is now a leading motivational humorist speaking to corporations, associations and healthcare professionals about the positive effects of a lighthearted attitude on workplace woes.

He is the founder of National Humor Month and the director of the Carmel Institute of Humor which sponsors public research and professional roundtables to explore laughter as a vital tool for wellness, productivity and the quality of life.

Larry lives on the California coast with his wife, Maryruth, who is also an author.

PINNACLE BOOKS HAS
SOMETHING FOR EVERYONE —

MAGICIANS, EXPLORERS, WITCHES AND CATS

THE HANDYMAN   (377-3, $3.95/$4.95)
He is a magician who likes hands. He likes their comfortable
shape and weight and size. He likes the portability of the hands
once they are severed from the rest of the ponderous body. Detec-
tive Lanark must discover who The Handyman is before more
handless bodies appear.

PASSAGE TO EDEN   (538-5, $4.95/$5.95)
Set in a world of prehistoric beauty, here is the epic story of a
courageous seafarer whose wanderings lead him to the ends of
the old world — and to the discovery of a new world in the rugged,
untamed wilderness of northwestern America.

BLACK BODY   (505-9, $5.95/$6.95)
An extraordinary chronicle, this is the diary of a witch, a journal
of the secrets of her race kept in return for not being burned for
her "sin." It is the story of Alba, that rarest of creatures, a white
witch: beautiful and able to walk in the human world undetected.

THE WHITE PUMA   (532-6, $4.95/NCR)
The white puma has recognized the men who deprived him of his
family. Now, like other predators before him, he has become a
man-hater. This story is a fitting tribute to this magnificent animal that stands for all living creatures that have become, through
man's carelessness, close to disappearing forever from the face of
the earth.

*Available wherever paperbacks are sold, or order direct from the
Publisher. Send cover price plus 50¢ per copy for mailing and
handling to Penguin USA, P.O. Box 999, c/o Dept. 17109,
Bergenfield, NJ 07621. Residents of New York and Tennessee
must include sales tax. DO NOT SEND CASH.*

INFORMATIVE—
COMPELLING—
SCINTILLATING—
NON-FICTION FROM PINNACLE TELLS THE TRUTH: